Beat Stress and Live Your Best
technique – Breathing Space
ten minutes. A group of pe
were asked to test, evaluate
is what they said:

> For anyone who has had the opportunity to meet the wonderfully charismatic, joyful, crazy and insightful Nikki Owen, you will love this book. I first worked with Nikki five years ago and she took me on a journey then. This adventure is not for people who feel somebody else needs to fix them; it's for the brave amongst us who know it sits with themselves. What Nikki does is help you get a perspective, and for the sceptics she explains the science behind Breathing Space. For those who know her, you'll hear her voice jumping out of the page, talking to you; you won't be surprised that she's taking you on another journey of self-discovery but deeper this time. For those who haven't met Nikki yet, hold on to your horses and let the journey begin!
>
> — **SUSIE LOTHERINGTON, INTERIM PROJECT MANAGER**

> Nikki is a true inspiration. Breathing Space is life changing and it's something I know I will practise forever. I couldn't recommend this highly enough.
>
> — **DONNA STANDING, RECRUITMENT PARTNER**

Breathing Space is unlike anything I have encountered before. Listening to your guided tracks made such an instant and positive difference to my mood and left me feeling lighter and full of energy.

— **SARITA BIRKS, NORTH WEST BREAKTHROUGH DEPUTY CHAIR**

I highly recommend Breathing Space if you feel you need to transform, heal or uplift your emotional wellbeing.

— **CELYNN MORIN, GLOBAL WELLBEING EXPERT**

In the midst of a pandemic, Breathing Space makes me feel comfortable with facing challenging and buried emotions that have held me back in my personal and work life. I assumed I had them for life. I was wrong! Breathing Space should be on prescription for everyone – it is truly amazing!

— **LIANE HARTLEY, MEMBER OF THE MAYOR OF LONDON'S INFRASTRUCTURE ADVISORY PANEL**

Breathing Space is a complete eye-opener. I didn't expect it to have the powerful effect that it does. My cognitive function seems to have improved and my thought processes have become clearer and sharper.

— **CARRIE OLIVER, EDUCATIONALIST**

I've always struggled with sleeping and it definitely helps me with my sleep. Breathing Space expands the possibilities for how well you can feel.

— **PIPPA HIGHAM, STUDENT**

Breathing Space has created a significant change and led me to making some significant professional decisions.

— **GILES WATKINS, AUTHOR, SPEAKER AND CONSULTANT**

In order for you to grow, you have to step outside your comfort zone because when you start expanding, when you start growing, opportunities start coming into your life and your life can completely change. Breathing Space is a completely different experience.

— **MAXINE KING, LIFE COACH**

When I feel exhausted I listen to Breathing Space and it's super energising. It just gets rid of all of that negative emotion and really sets me up for the day. Being analytical makes meditation challenging but with Breathing Space I can't possibly think about anything else.

— **LISA KERR, CHIEF OPERATING OFFICER**

When I started Breathing Space, I approached it with a curious and open mind. I didn't know what to expect. I have to say that it immediately blew me away.

— **CLAIRE CHANT, YOGA TEACHER**

Breathing Space allows you to feel like a better person, and you become more tolerant. At times like these, being more tolerant is a wonderful thing because we're all under immense pressure.

— **ANDY REID, BUSINESS OWNER**

I have been feeling amazing since [practising Breathing Space]. I'm so much calmer and I feel really peaceful and a lot more able to cope. Breathing Space is amazing – Nikki J. Owen is the Joe Wicks of the mind therapy world!

— **KARAN TATTERSFIELD, HR DIRECTOR AND SINGLE MUM**

I can't describe it, it felt amazing. I just felt lighter. I felt that I could breathe better. Before doing Breathing Space I was starting to get a bit of anxiety in my chest – that just went within the first session. I'm at home and I am busy and I never stop. Breathing Space gets my head right for the morning.

— **KELLY HENLEY, PERSONAL TRAINER**

Frankly I haven't seen anything like Breathing Space anywhere else. It's kept me tolerant; it's kept me kind, loving, compassionate. It really has made such an enormous difference to how I feel at this time.

— **WENDY SHAND, ENTREPRENEUR**

Breathing Space takes Nikki up another level – if that were possible! It's brilliant; it works. Grab it with both hands – you'll thank me afterwards.

— **SIMON LESTER, CEO**

As a terrible overthinker and a poor sleeper, it is making such a difference! Mind is calmer, sleep is better and energy levels are starting to restore. It may seem a bit bonkers but I do recommend trying it!

— **ISABELLE JARMIN, COMMUNICATIONS, PROJECT & EVENTS MANAGER**

Breathing Space has been a big influence on both my personal and business life. I would highly recommend giving Breathing Space a try and see the huge benefits it can make to both your personal and private life.

— **MARK CHIVERS, SALES MANAGER**

A real innovation. As someone who has implemented Breathing Space, I can tell you, it absolutely works!

— **DIANE YATES, HEAD OF LEADERSHIP & EXECUTIVE DEVELOPMENT**

From the first Breathing Space session, I immediately felt a profound impact. The best endorsement for Breathing Space will be my kids and my wife who have all said how much calmer I am. If you've struggled with meditation before, then I suggest you try Breathing Space.

— STEVE MCCONNELL, BUSINESS OWNER

For me Breathing Space has helped me release 'stuff' that has been with me for years. I have found it very liberating. Give it a go and rediscover yourself.

— SHARON BAXTER, HEAD OF CUSTOMER ACCOUNT MANAGEMENT

Breathing Space has definitely changed me. I love myself more, my headaches have stopped and I sleep much better at night.

— INESA WILLIAMS, COMMERCIAL FINANCE MANAGER

BEAT STRESS AND LIVE YOUR BEST LIFE

A STRESSBUSTING TECHNIQUE THAT
WORKS IN 10 MINUTES

NIKKI J. OWEN

STRESSBUSTING EXPERT

Copyright © 2021 by Nikki J. Owen

All rights reserved.

No part of this book may be reproduced in any form or by any electronic or mechanical means, including information storage and retrieval systems, without written permission from the author, except for the use of brief quotations in a book review.

Editing and typesetting: www.preparetopublish.com

CONTENTS

Warning	xv
Foreword	xvii
Prologue	1
1. The path less travelled	3
2. There are no mistakes	9
3. Blocks to happiness	23
4. Are you surviving or thriving?	41
5. Reality is not real!	51
6. Who are you?	67
7. What is Breathing Space?	81
8. Learning the technique	89
9. Technology into 'mindology'	115
10. Your journey to your best life	123
Key people, events and terms	127
Bibliography	135
Acknowledgements	141
About the Author	143

"Nikki J. Owen is the Joe Wicks of the mind therapy world!"
  – Karan Tattersfield, HR director

"Life is not measured by the number of breaths we take, but by the moments that take our breath away."
– Vicki Corona, 1989 Tahitian Choreographies

To my daughter Rosie, you took my breath away on the day you were born. I dedicate this book, based on my life's work, to the miracle of you.

WARNING

This book explains a stressbusting technique referred to as Breathing Space. This practice is not suitable for anyone who has high blood pressure, is, or thinks they may be, pregnant, breastfeeding or has any serious illness. Breathing Space is not recommended for people who are fasting or are under 18. Please visit your local medical practitioner for their expert advice before you start Breathing Space.

FOREWORD
NEBEL CROWHURST, PEOPLE AND CULTURE DIRECTOR

Nikki Owen... thank you! Thank you for the great work you have done and continue to do. Thank you for opening my eyes to such an exciting new world. Most of all, thank you for becoming a lifelong friend. People like you are few and far between, and I feel incredibly fortunate that our paths were destined to cross.

I met Nikki when the organisation I was working for at that time commissioned her to deliver a piece of work that supported our sales approach. I was part of the team delivering this initiative and I knew immediately there was something very special, unique and captivating about her.

Spanning three large and well-known organisations, we have worked on a variety of pioneering projects together; from high-impact talent and leadership programmes, to 121 executive breakthrough sessions, to the exciting new work of Breathing Space. Over time I have had the pleasure of watching how Nikki's work has developed and evolved, continually taking on new and creative approaches that enable individuals, teams and organisations to thrive.

My own breakthrough came when I participated in one of Nikki's transformational programmes. I remember the experience vividly. The room we were in, the feeling of excited curiosity amongst the group, the feeling of lightness as I began to open my eyes to the world in a very different way. It was during this period that I grew to really respect Nikki as a professional in her field and began to develop a personal connection that has continued to grow. Sometimes people come into your life at just the right moment, for just the right reason. Nikki is definitely one of those people. Her sense of intuition and awareness is like no other. Her ability to read the tiniest of reactions and get a feel for what you are feeling is inexplicable. Nikki is more intuitive than the most attuned empath.

Besides my personal learning through Nikki's extraordinary work, in my roles within organisations I have been privileged to share her work with others. I have had a career working with people through learning and development, organisational design and human resources. My passion is to provide interventions that give people the ability to be the very best versions of themselves. This ensures that they deliver their work to the highest standard and in turn contribute to the success of their organisation. By incorporating Nikki's programmes into my leadership and talent solutions, I have been able to provide something far greater and more impactful than any traditional, corporate offering. I am proud to have been able to elevate what's perceived to be trite 'management and leadership development' into something that genuinely supports people to live an authentic life from a position of powerful flow.

Beat Stress and Live Your Best Life gives the reader an opportunity to benefit personally from Nikki's unique blend of transformational coaching. This book is a masterclass that offers you a gateway into becoming a better version of yourself. It takes you on a journey that shows you how to feel happier, healthier and more energised. Whatever the type of work that you do, or even if you don't work, *Beat Stress and*

Live Your Best Life will convince you that your potential is limitless.

We are living in a world of constant change and uncertainty. A world that is shifting around us at an exponential rate. We need to build on our resilience, coping mechanisms and our ability to deal with the unknown. Some choose to do this through the practice of mindfulness, some through yoga and others through coaching and mentoring. For me, it is about a blend of all of these. Why not be in a position to possess a toolkit that you can draw upon at any given time? This is where I see Breathing Space, a tool that I can benefit from whenever I need to let go of the stressors and anxieties of life.

Breath is a powerful remedy. When we use our breath, we can calm ourselves, re-energise and re-focus when we need to. When this is blended with releasing and behavioural change techniques, the results are instantaneous. Breathing Space is the evolution of years of work and research by Nikki. The depth of this profound practice is life changing.

Thank you again Nikki, for being the pioneer, the creator, the influencer – and for sharing your work with the world.

Namasté.

PROLOGUE

The room was unbearably hot. The feeling of impending death felt heavy and oppressive. The man in the single bed was dehydrated and skeletal, his rasping breath echoing around the room.

"Dad!" I whispered as I held his hand. "Dad, I think it's time."

Dad opened his eyes with an alertness that seemed utterly discordant with the state of his physical body. We had talked about the moment when the syringe driver filled with morphine would be administered. He knew that it would release him from pain and ease his passing. Yet we both accepted that it would send him into a deep sleeping state where conversation with loved ones would no longer be possible.

I felt an unbearable sadness as I remembered the vibrant man my father had once been. He was an extraordinary character who could evoke frustration and love in equal measure. His drive to create a better life for his family meant that he never gave up on anything he believed to be in his family's best interest. This fighting spirit resulted in his qualification as a chartered accountant – an incredible achievement for a poor working-class lad from a deprived London suburb, who was described as 'pretty useless'.

As his career flourished, he met and fell in love with Pam, a woman he never stopped loving. Together they had three children. I'm the oldest, then there is my sister Sally and our younger brother Johnnie. My parents, Ed and Pam, created an idyllic family home that was the epicentre of Dad's life for over 20 years. Then his life took a twisted turn for the worse when our beautiful home was deliberately burned down and the monster that lived amongst us nearly destroyed our family.

I wanted his last few moments of consciousness to be full of joy. I wanted him to remember the happy times, not the painful times. I wanted him to feel a deep peace that went beyond his surrender to the morphine. I wanted him to feel soothed and happy.

"Dad, you've achieved so much in your life. Out of everything you've done – what are you most proud of?"

Dad smiled and his whole expression softened. "Saving you."

1

THE PATH LESS TRAVELLED

Do you need saving? I don't necessarily mean physically, but do you feel lost in the maelstrom of your emotions or weary from the chaos of living in this uncertain world?

Are you feeling the burdens of extreme pressure? Have you noticed that you're experiencing more stress, tension and anxiety? Does life feel like a constant battle, fighting a continual stream of problems and challenges? Have you got to a point in life where you feel weary, disillusioned and resentful about where you're at right now?

Workplace surveys have identified that 79% of employees are now suffering from stress. Are you one of these people? Have you noticed that if you've retained your job through the Covid-19 pandemic there is a general expectation that, regardless of what goes on in the world, you should be feeling lucky, upbeat, positive and optimistic? But many of us are struggling to a greater or lesser degree with the adjustment of home-working, endless hours of Zoom meetings, childcare issues, social isolation and worrying about the future. It's hardly surprising that a general fatigue has set in, particularly as we face the prospect of adjusting to living under the omnipotent shadow of a global pandemic.

When you feel stressed, your hypothalamus, a tiny region at the base of your brain, sets off an internal alarm system. Cortisol is released into your system and activates your fight-or-flight response. Cortisol is not supposed to remain in your system for long because it alters immune system responses and suppresses the digestive, reproductive and growth systems.

When you feel good your brain releases chemicals such as serotonin and oxytocin that perpetuate this feeling of balance, strengthen your immune system and ensure good health.

You deserve the best

Stress has a funny way of sucking the joy out of life. It taints your technicolour world with sepia monotones. Stress can creep up on you slowly or it can jump out at unexpected moments, shouting so loudly that you become deafened to your potential to feel truly happy.

Can you remember a time when the adventure of life felt enthralling and you were giddy about its potential for pleasure? Growing up, did you see a road paved with riches, fairy-tale endings, a cottage by the sea with roses and a white picket fence? At some point in your life were your childhood illusions of rich possibilities shattered? Have you noticed a tedium entering your life as you get older? Have you taken the awe and wonder for granted in the monotony of your Groundhog Days? Have you become inhibited, stopped laughing out loud or screeching with delight? When did you last splash in a puddle? Many people – and maybe you're one of those people – have learned to take care, take precautions, be sensible, tough it out, put on a brave face and keep on going. For many people, pain, hardship, betrayal, fear, injustice and sorrow cause them to lower their expectations from life. They begin to compromise, to settle for less than they really want. They have accepted the mundane as okay. Have you noticed how many people use language such as "I'm fine" or "I'm not too bad"? Their passion for life has become muted. Are you busy being busy? You work hard, you try your best, you make mistakes, you learn, you change, you grow old. Sometimes in this cycle of life, you feel happy and satisfied – but, too often, it's a noticeable exception rather than the norm. Have your hopes and aspirations been ground into a dust that has blinded you to the beauty of your potential to feel truly happy? Sometimes life feels too much and it's hard to believe that you do deserve the best that life can offer.

Life is your playground

This isn't the time to run from yourself. This is the time to stop and stand still. This isn't the moment to ignore the desires of your heart. This is the moment to be fully present with who you are. When you stop expecting more from life, you end up with less. When you accept the ordinary, you turn your back on your extraordinariness. When you put up with the pain, you dampen your spirit and disconnect from the enchantment of what is really out there. Many people are walking around carrying multiple layers of conflict that they have either suppressed or repressed: are you one of them? When you know how to liberate yourself from emotional suffering, you'll experience that life is your playground. A playground for fun, laughter and endless joy. We can learn so much from children. They see the world through a psychedelic lens. As children grow, this lens becomes dirty as the grime of disappointment lingers in the shadows, unacknowledged but always present. It's not life that is disappointing, you just need to clean the lens that you're viewing your life through.

Cleaning up

This book helps you to see the world through fresh eyes. The over-intellectualising, the processed food, the addiction to Facebook, the mind-numbing pastime of TV; all induce a fog that stops your world from gleaming. When you know how to beat stress, your entire world becomes different. Your birthright is to feel bliss in all its glory. You deserve the best in every aspect of your life. When you love and accept all aspects of the person you have become and treat yourself with respect, your energy will attract all that your heart desires. The universe loves you and wants to support you in your quest for a joyful existence.

Two different pathways

Imagine two pathways stretching out ahead of you. One path has been walked on by thousands of people because it is well defined and easy to walk. The branches of the trees and the brambles from the undergrowth have been cut back and it looks like a good, safe decision, a comforting choice, to walk in this direction. The other pathway is barely visible. You can tell that not many people, if any, have walked this way before. The gnarled branches from wizened trees have entangled with the branches from other trees, making it difficult to see that far ahead. Stinging nettles, wild heather and ivy have been left untamed for years, happy to grow with a freedom that obscures any sense of clear direction. Yet take a closer look at this pathway. Look beyond the darkness and, if you remain still and quiet for a moment, you'll see countless rays of sunlight that trickle through the dense canopy overhead. Bright beams of energy illuminating the shady path. Butterflies with vibrant scarlet wings dance along these beams, caught in the spotlight, basking in the glory of their iridescent beauty. Every aspect of you is projected out into the surrounding woodland as you begin to see its true beauty. Nature creates perfection with every tiny nuance of creation itself. This is the path less travelled (excuse the plagiarism from M. Scott Peck's title of his great book, *The Road Less Travelled*). This is the path to joy, freedom, happiness and deep contentment. Even though this path brings great rewards, not many people are prepared to enter into the shadows and walk this path. Those that do will experience the greatest adventure and discover that everything we want already exists within us.

Let me help you on your journey

I know that you're about to experience a miraculous change in the way you feel. Our paths have connected and, as we begin this journey together, I ask you to keep your mind open and remain curious about exploring the depths of your potential. At times I will navigate you through the dark, rocky terrain of your perceived limitations, your challenges, the emotional traumas you've experienced in your life and the pressures that you are carrying on a daily basis. You may get angry with some of the principles you read about. You may find parts of this book cause you to feel uncomfortable as your mind becomes stretched by new ways of perceiving things around and within you. This journey we are taking ultimately leads you to a place of serenity, joy and happiness. A world that feels exciting, satisfying and nurturing. An environment where compassion appears to flow with wild abundance and every moment feels important and imbued with a magical quality.

A simple structure

The first six chapters give you an overview about why you experience your life as you do. But there is a difference between knowing something and living it. Which is why from chapter seven onwards you'll be introduced to Breathing Space, a stressbusting technique that supports you to live your best life. It is the culmination of my 30 years of study, research and experience. If I explain Breathing Space too soon, your level of commitment to integrating it into your daily routine will be compromised. I ask you to read this book from the beginning, in readiness for the miraculous change you will undoubtably create for yourself. My intention is to illuminate your awareness, transform your thinking and guide you towards your inner extraordinary. It's time to start our journey together. Are you ready for this?

2

THERE ARE NO MISTAKES

I remember a night when I was seven and struggling to breathe. It was about three o'clock in the morning and my parents, brother and sister were asleep. I was propped up with pillows and a bad asthma attack had kept me awake because every breath was a struggle. The fear that I couldn't absorb enough air to take my next breath was overwhelming. My pink ballerina pyjamas were drenched with sweat and my fists were clenched with so much 'efforting'. I had been crying silently for the past hour and I really wanted my mum and dad with me. But I couldn't do anything or shout out because every breath was such hard work. I have never felt so small and alone as I did in this moment.

For many years afterwards I experienced high levels of anxiety if I woke up during the night hours. My unconscious mind continued to hold on to my childhood fear of not being able to breathe, and this created so much stress.

What defines you?

My own life experience has taught me so much. Everything you have experienced has defined the person you are today.

Your struggles have created the opportunity, to experience a better version of you. It is tempting to reflect back on life and feel saddened by the pain you've suffered, frustrated about the circumstances that caused your hopes to fall in the harsh reality of life. But there are no mistakes in life. Only lessons that you and I may have accepted or rejected.

Every trauma contains a nugget of gold

When you reflect back across your life, you may recognise that the hardest times caused you to grow and become a better person. When you stop judging yourself or your past, you can access wisdom and valuable learnings from your experiences. This may take you a short time, a longer time, or you may never see any good aspects about what happened to you. Holding on to your pain and blaming other people for the suffering you endured keeps you in a dark place. This leads to stress, depression, dysfunctional behaviours and physical/mental health issues. Clearly, not the right conditions for you to feel happy and joyful!

If you were to tell the younger me that the night when I battled to breathe would inform my life's work, I wouldn't have been able to hear you. I wasn't receptive to anything except the struggle for my own survival.

There are no mistakes in life.

Being honest about the person you have become

Your life experiences have created the person you are today. You may love and accept who you are or loathe who you have become. When you judge an aspect of you that you don't like, you damage yourself. You create a need to hide what you perceive as 'the bad version of you' and it takes energy to hide your shadow self. This creates tension in your body and affects the way that you breathe. You begin to orientate away from who you really are and towards the type of person you think you should be. This switch in direction creates inauthenticity. A part of you is sacrificed because you've judged that part as not good enough. If you blame your past for how you are now, or who you are now, you've blocked your potential for joy. You've blocked your ability to see that your past has equipped you with a unique set of experiences that can be expressed in a positive way for the benefit of humanity.

There are no mistakes in life.

Stress manipulates behaviour

I had pushed down the stress of not being able to breathe when I was seven, and over the years this inner tension created an emotional and physical imbalance that changed my state of mind and my behaviour. On 22 December 1978, aged 18, I was in the dock at the Old Bailey, charged with arson, endangering life and intent to kill my mother. During my early teens my behaviour had become increasingly violent, culminating in burning down the family home. I was sent to Holloway Prison and because of my volatile rages I was incarcerated in solitary confinement. Years of self-harming, a shaved head, scars from slashed wrists and a 20kg weight gain had transformed me into 'a monster'. Up until my early teens I had been part of a loving family and a talented dancer who used to do part-time modelling to earn a bit of cash. My parents couldn't understand what had triggered their eldest and gentle daughter to suddenly appear violent, irrational and without self-control. They decided to invite eight of the UK's most well-respected psychiatrists to examine me in Holloway Prison.

There are no mistakes in life.

Maniacal psychopath – destination Broadmoor

These eight reports were chilling and left no hope for my recovery. I was described as 'Incurably insane, a danger to society and a maniacal psychopath'. They collectively recommended that I serve a life sentence in Broadmoor, the hospital for the criminally insane. When the prison governor at Holloway told me about the application for me to go to Broadmoor, I felt the tiny flicker of hope within me extinguish. My cell was small and dark. My prison dress was made from indestructible material so I couldn't hang myself. Even though I was given a mattress to sleep on, I wasn't allowed a blanket, so I felt continually cold. Twice a day I was fed through a hatch in the door because I was deemed 'too dangerous' for the wardens to enter my cell. I was held in solitary confinement for several months, only being allowed out once a week so that I could write a letter home. I stopped being Nicola Jane Owen and became 'Prisoner DO2572'.

There are no mistakes in life.

Fear locks you up

The real confinement was happening inside my head as it happens inside other people's heads. Fear causes you to close down and lock yourself away from perceived dangers. The more scared you feel, the more you bury of yourself. How can you feel joy in a dark place full of limitations, stress and anxiety? As your fear starts to affect your body, you'll notice that the tension from fear creates a tension in breath. Your brain is neuroplastic and malleable, so you emotionally adjust to these damaging conditions and your breathing pattern is adjusted accordingly. Your breathing has now become *fear breathing*, which is typically shallow and fast. Your breath adds to the feeling of *fear*, but the pattern has already been established. You normalise these conditions and you forget that your natural essence is pure joy. You start to forget what happiness feels like and become numb to the anguish that eats away at your heart.

There are no mistakes in life.

Severe hormone imbalance

My parents were told to forget about me and to focus their love on their other two children, my younger brother and sister; but their love for me was stronger than their own despair and they began to explore where my apparent 'madness' had come from. My father's quest to save me from a life behind bars inspired my mum and together they discovered that my abnormal behaviour was linked to my menstrual cycle. In the days before the internet and Google searches, they spent hours in the local library and discovered a specialist in hormonal imbalances. Gynaecologist and female hormone expert Dr Katharina Dalton agreed to visit me in prison and diagnosed a severe lack of progesterone resulting in extreme premenstrual syndrome (PMS). The prison authorities agreed to take me off the high doses of sedatives that kept me docile and started me on progesterone treatment. Within three weeks I experienced a remarkable change in how I felt and how I wanted to behave. As part of my new defence, I was revisited by the same eight psychiatrists whose reports had previously been so damning. They described my transformation as "nothing short of a miracle".

There are no mistakes in life.

Is your life out of balance?

My hormone imbalance was an extreme example of the damage that is created from physical or emotional imbalance. When you work too hard, your body tells you that it wants to rest. If you ignore the cries from your body, you'll experience an increase in your general suffering. Imbalance is not a problem if it is experienced for a day or so, but if your life is out of balance for a long time, your natural equilibrium is thrown into disarray. You begin to fight the natural flow of your life. This fight becomes imprinted onto your breath pattern and you fight for every breath.

Making legal history

As my trial approached, I was introduced to my barrister, Mr Addezio, who had agreed to use PMS as a mitigating factor as my defence. His peers believed that it was an impossible case to win because PMS had never been used as a legal defence. Just before my trial started, Mr Addezio visited me in the holding cell at the Old Bailey. He told me that if the judge didn't accept PMS as a mitigating factor, I would be facing 12–15 years in prison and could therefore be in prison until my thirties. The courtroom was packed after the press discovered that an unusual precedent was occurring in Court 13. Mr Addezio fought hard to save me from a life behind bars. His defence worked and my case made legal history and I became a free woman. I was bewildered by what had just happened and terrified about the future.

There are no mistakes in life.

Sometimes it's hard to let go

Several weeks after my dramatic release from prison, I kept reliving the horrors of solitary confinement. I was scared to leave the house because the press kept publishing sensationalist articles. People I once knew would cross the road rather than have to walk past me. I was haunted by what had happened as I repeated the trauma of my experiences over and over again in my thoughts. My mind was still keeping me imprisoned, as I continually beat myself up for the terrible things I had done to my family. Even though our home had been rebuilt, I was aware that my parents watched me warily. My childhood asthma had returned, created by the stress I was still carrying from my past.

There are no mistakes in life.

The fight for survival

The more miserable I was, the more I attracted miserable people, and together we found temporary solace from drinking in the darkness of life. I coped by rejecting my emotions and giving my heart an emotional anaesthetic. The tsunami of suppressed emotional undercurrents still raged within me although I felt emotionally numb. I learned how to stop crying, in total ignorance that my tears were falling inwards. I pushed myself hard and took on work so I could distract myself from the stream of incessant thoughts. I found temporary respite in alcohol, food, obsessive exercise, casual sex and sometimes drugs. Work became the way I could create a little self-worth, but I always pushed myself too hard. My pallor took on a greyish hue; my neck, shoulders and back felt tense and heavy under the burdens I was still carrying from my past. My weight fluctuated dramatically: I either gained weight and looked bloated or lost weight and looked gaunt. Sleep became my enemy, another nightly battle that left me waking up feeling exhausted before the day started. My immune system was shot to pieces and I got many allergies, colds, coughs, skin rashes, aches in my joints and lower back pain. My asthma attacks were held at bay with a Ventolin inhaler, but I noticed that I was cautious about taking deep breaths. One day I woke up crippled with anxiety. With horror I realised that I couldn't think straight. Even the smallest task felt overwhelming. My daily routine was a dangerous minefield and I felt exhausted from being on high alert all the time. The growing panic, the mounting despair, felt like a cancerous growth eating away at the person that was once me.

There are no mistakes in life.

Listen to your body

In moments like this you are being given a powerful message. Mental toughness is not about protecting yourself from the onslaught of life. It is trusting that the world you inhabit loves and supports you. It is having faith that your emotions are there to guide you. When you feel a negative emotion, listen to the message because you are walking the wrong path. Your courage is enabled when you allow your vulnerability to show. It is your softness that becomes your true strength. Whatever difficulties, obstacles or challenges you are dealing with right now, this time will pass. I couldn't change my past and it was that realisation that led me to an important decision. I could only change myself. Despite being full of anger and self-hatred, I wanted to live a better life, I wanted to start my life over again and I wanted a second chance. A strong desire for healing my emotional wounds to liberate myself from inner torment and suffering has taken me on a fascinating journey.

There are no mistakes in life.

My journey of healing

I rejected 'talking-based' therapies because reliving my past kept me trapped in my past. In 1999 I trained in neuro-linguistic programming (NLP) and completed my trainer's training in Orange County, Florida in 2000 with Tad James and David Shephard. Paul McKenna mentored me in 1993 and introduced me to Michael Breen, who I worked with informally. I've also studied briefly with Richard Bandler, who

I adore because of his wantonness in experimenting with different ways of thinking. If I'm honest, when I did my trainer's training in NLP, I felt I lost myself and felt programmed into becoming an NLP clone of everybody else. Whilst feeling grateful for my NLP training, I worked hard to reconnect with my own authentic essence. I'm a qualified hypnotherapist and Time Line Therapy trainer and blend these tools with Emotional Freedom Techniques, or 'tapping' as it's more frequently known. I studied Matrix Reimprinting with its founder, Karl Dawson. In 2009 I commenced my reiki training and worked through the different levels until I became a reiki master. My ability to work with subtle energies grew exponentially when I studied with a gifted psychic, Paul Wayman, for two years. One of my career highlights occurred in 2010, when an international broadcasting corporation invited me to provide political commentary on the UK's first live TV debate between the political party leaders of the time. Despite my presence perplexing Stephen Haseler (a professor of government and author of many books on British politics), I was well received when I analysed Gordon Brown, David Cameron and Nick Clegg's non-verbal communication. My sensory awareness and my ability to read people within a few seconds has proved a big hit with my clients.

The 'weird and whacky'

In 2006 I became an accredited fire-walking instructor. After burning my feet pretty badly, I realised the power of the mind over the body and could successfully fire-walk without any burns. I've experienced a heightened level of consciousness during a sweat lodge that helped me to release fears that I'd held on to since my teens. I've given myself deliberate hypothermia with cryotherapy to prove my mental toughness and the power of positive self-talk. For years I sought to tame my thoughts and practised a mantra-based meditation process after studying with the charismatic Will Williams. When my 'monkey mind' began to quieten down, I noticed my awareness was sharper. I learned how to breathe correctly (most people don't breathe properly) and learned transformational breathwork with the Breath Guru, Alan Dolan. When I discovered that Albert Einstein was an advocate of dowsing, a friend suggested that I train with the British Society of Dowsers. If you're not familiar with dowsing, it brings that which is hidden up into your conscious awareness. As an accomplished dowser, I still use dowsing with clients to demonstrate how positive and negative thought patterns affect energy levels. After two divorces, I realised that love and understanding is diminished when either tries to change the other. In the absence of love and acceptance for your partner, judgement and criticism begin to surface. I sought help from the Relationship Wizard, Andrew Wallas, and his wife, Anna Pasternak, and had couples' therapy all by myself!

Deepening my awareness

My friend Claire has introduced me to a number of interesting yoga-based experiences over the years that have deepened my meditation practice. I discovered kundalini yoga after a visit to Beachyjax in Yorkshire, and this unusual style of yoga is an essential part of my daily routine. I released years of unprocessed anger with free-style movement as I danced to Gabrielle Roth's 5Rhythms.

My friend and spiritual mentor Sue introduced me to a myriad of esoteric practices over the years, including Vajrayana Buddhism during a week's one-to-one retreat. This profoundly deepened my knowledge about consciousness, ultimate reality and compassion.

My hallucinogenic adventure

In November 2019, friends Jacqui and Dave persuaded me to travel to Costa Rica and experience ayahuasca. This hallucinogenic, plant-based medicine has been used by indigenous people for over four thousand years for emotional and physical healing. It was mind blowing and had a huge impact on my self-worth by giving me a better understanding of the person I have become and why. Ayahuasca took me to some pretty dark places before showing me that the most important relationship we have is with ourselves.

Your journey of healing

Many areas of incoherence in your own life will be the echoes of repressed or suppressed emotions that you didn't process and release when you were younger. This creates a layer of stress that can only be released when you are able to express those buried emotions. To live life to the fullest requires you to work on your emotional baggage and the younger parts of you that are crying out for healing. Without a willingness to heal your emotional wounds your capacity for happiness will be muted. The more you persevere with releasing your stored emotional baggage, the lighter you'll feel and the more satisfaction you'll get from life. There will always be something to work on so accept continual learning as nonchalantly as you accept brushing your teeth every day.

Victorious or victim?

I find great joy in witnessing the transformation of others that have resulted from their willingness to address their stress levels and commit to beating it. I feel incredibly lucky that my life's purpose was shaped early on in my life. I've had decades of experience and helped thousands of people from all types of backgrounds. My clients are courageous because they open themselves to feeling vulnerable. I love the moment when they finally acknowledge that just being true to themselves is enough. Even though the path to the woman I am today has not been an easy one, I have learned to accept myself for who I am and have found a way to make peace with my painful past. It doesn't serve me to become a victim of my trauma and it doesn't serve you to become a victim of yours.

There are no mistakes in life.

Your precious life

Your life has probably not been smooth sailing all the time. The choice is whether you have become hardened by life's knocks or have chosen to expand into greater awareness. It's not about toughening up. It's about softening up. Think of two balls. One is made from concrete. It should be indestructible but if dropped from a certain height it will smash to pieces. The other ball is made from foam, and even if an articulated lorry drives over it, it will always bounce back to its original form. When you look back on your own past and judge it as bad or painful, you are condemning yourself to a continuation of more suffering. It is your judgement of your past, or your present, or your future, that is the real problem. Every time you relive a bad experience, it keeps it alive. Releasing the pain from your past allows happiness to grow. Your life is incredibly precious. Sometimes in the chaos of everyday living you may forget that your life is a gift. It might take a global pandemic, redundancy, divorce, bereavement or a serious illness to give you a wake-up call that every moment of your time here on Planet Earth is valuable and important. You don't know what your future holds, but your point of power is how you choose to experience your life right now. It's not helpful to hold on to the past and ruin your life for years. It's not helpful to worry about your future. When you surrender to the natural way that your life unfolds and accept that you are always learning, always growing, always expanding, your life gets easier to live. Happiness and all that you desire exists within you right now.

There are no mistakes in life.

3

BLOCKS TO HAPPINESS

Being human attracts a lot of suffering. You have desires to acquire something, or to feel a certain way. If the things you desire don't manifest for you, then you experience suffering. If someone you love dies, your grief causes you to suffer. If you imagine a future possibility that makes you feel anxious then you suffer. It is part of the condition of being a human being. If you suffer, then how can you possibly be happy? The first challenge about 'humanness' is coping with your emotions. These can feel wonderful, rewarding and uplifting, or they bring heaps of emotional pain. As you reflect on your own life, did you have an expectation that life would be one positive experience after another? But the truth is that you have suffered. Perhaps you've had your heart broken, been kept awake at night worrying about money or felt helpless after watching the evening news. Maybe a family member is going through a tough time or you have children and are continually worried about keeping them safe. The false expectation that life should be easy makes the suffering even tougher to endure, which is why so many people harden their hearts or give themselves an *emotional anaesthetic*.

You CAN live in paradise

Imagine living in paradise, where the sun shines and nothing ever goes wrong. Initially you delight in your luxuriant living, although if you're honest, the continual *sameness* of this luxury causes you to want more from your life, maybe the odd adventure. What satisfied you at first no longer gives you that same warm glow. You find a bigger, more opulent house nearer to the sea and you get that warm glow again and believe that now you'll be happy forever. It doesn't take long before you are so used to the spectacular views and the sparkling ocean that you no longer see it or appreciate it as you become distracted with Facebook and posting filtered selfies of yourself on Instagram! If you continue to seek paradise outside of yourself, then it eventually isn't enough to stop your suffering. Inherently within you is a desire to grow and expand. If you don't do anything to grow proactively, then life has a funny way of doing it for you. Think back to the biggest difficulties you've experienced and notice what you learned, how it changed your perspective, how it gave you emotional depth. When your life doesn't go as you want it to, you can either get irritated or you can smile in the knowledge that something within you is letting you know that it's time to go back to the School of Life again because there are important lessons waiting to be learned.

Loss can enrich your life

I was recently travelling by train to attend a day of personal development with my 'Fabulous Women's Group'. I know this is a strange name to call our group, but we are an eclectic bunch of weird and whacky females who share a common passion for exploring the Self. My plan was to travel to Birmingham afterwards for an overnight stay before returning home. At some point in my journey I left my suitcase on a train. It was crammed with some of my favourite clothes. Sparkly trainers and a red leather skirt, beauty gadgets that resembled robotic toys and some unique jewellery that I had amassed over the years. Knickers from ASDA (no great loss), an old copy of my autobiography that is now out of print, and a beautiful crystal ball. Usually I hold little attachment to material 'stuff' but for some reason I felt bereft that I had not taken care of some of my most cherished possessions. Sometimes 'angels' appear in unusual forms. When I phoned the Great Northern lost property phone line, I got through to the amazingly helpful 'Max'. He tracked down the different trains I was on and finally reunited me with my suitcase. I realised how easy it is to take things for granted. I gained much more than my suitcase that day. I realised that the thought of loss caused me emotional pain and that appreciation of what you love can sometimes only be realised when it's gone.

Life is about contrast

In the relentless quest for happiness, you seldom realise that the hunger for what you crave is created because of its opposite. How can you appreciate the flame of a single candle if it is held up against the sun? How can you know what you want unless you experience what you don't want? Sometimes a lack of appreciation for what is taken for granted, such as your health, a job, a relationship, may cause a sense of entitlement. Only when it is lost or missing do you feel a deeper appreciation for that which you once had.

Desire is a natural programme

In general our society programmes us to continually desire more. Such is your appetite for bigger and better that you may sometimes fall out of love with what you already have, and what you once experienced as enchanting now looks grey and drab. This is the fleeting nature of happiness. Researchers on emotion have long known about something called the 'hedonic treadmill'. You work very hard to reach a goal, anticipating the happiness it will bring. Unfortunately, after a brief fix you quickly slide back to your ordinary way of being and start chasing the next thing you believe will finally make you happy.

Chaos brings expansion

In the moments when your life feels insane and out of control, you may grasp a lesson of such significance that it changes your destiny. Gratitude and appreciation cause your heart to sing as your perception of the world evolves into a breathtaking vista of multicoloured beauty. The hero within you is shaped by failure and your unquenchable thirst for life. Challenges can define you and enable you to return to your natural simplicity with a deep appreciation of what you once left behind. Be thankful for what you have and be grateful for what you have lost. It is in the losing that you learn about what's really important to you. It's in the losing that you learn to accept the curve balls of life. It's only when you lose do you have the opportunity to experience acceptance that life is what it is now. You learn more about yourself when you are faced with the challenge of loss. With the right spirit you can optimise the learning within each loss to experience a deeper sense of gratitude for the mystery that is you.

Emotional attachment

If you have become attached to having things just as you want them, then you're going to continue to suffer because nothing in life ever stays the same. I remember having a relationship with a man who wasn't particularly into me. I would live for the moments that we were together. Yet even whilst I was with him, I was worrying about the time he would be leaving. My days and nights were full of emotional angst as I twisted myself into knots of despair because he wasn't being the type of boyfriend that I wanted him to be. My happiness became conditional on seeing him. I was so blinded by my own emotional attachment to this man that I failed to realise how unhappy I was. Many people attach conditions to their happiness: "I'll be happy when I lose this weight", "I'll be happy when I've got this new car", "I'll be happy when he moves in with me." It's foolhardy to stake your own happiness on someone or something else, because you can't control people and you can't control everything that's going on around you. To experience true happiness requires you to stop looking outside of yourself for a cause to feel happy about. Instead, when you look within yourself and find your happiness there, you'll always possess it, regardless of what's going on in your life.

Your childhood programming

When you were born you entered the world in a hypnogogic state. Your unconscious mind was wide open and grasping to learn how to interact with this whole new world. You were highly suggestable and 'ripe' for programming. You observed, recorded and downloaded the behavioural programmes from your parents or the people that raised you. Your unconscious mind didn't care whether these programmes were positive or damaging; they were just what was on offer at the time. By the time you got to around six or seven years old you were much more aware of your behaviour and how it impacted upon others. You knew that if you did what your parents wanted, they would praise you and express their happiness. Maybe they would give you hugs or sweet and sugary food. If you didn't behave in the way they wanted, you may have experienced negative consequences. Perhaps they shouted at you, made you sit on the 'naughty step', sent you to your room or confiscated your favourite toy. I am not judging your parents or anyone else's parents, because people generally try to do the best that they can and are affected by how they've been programmed. Early on in life you formed your ideas about what is 'good' and what is 'bad'. These ideas have developed over time into behavioural programmes, beliefs and attitudes and have impacted in the way your body moves. Look at the jutting chin of an individual who is stubborn. Watch a person with low self-confidence: their shoulders are rounded and their head drops forward. It is estimated by therapists, counsellors and cellular biologists that over 80% of adult behaviour is programmed in childhood. Most of the behaviour you demonstrate as your adult self is not your behaviour (you've emulated your parents' behaviour) and is probably hampering your ability to feel happy.

Blissful unawareness

If your parents were fastidious about their appearance, chances are that you will be too. If your father was aloof, detached and struggled to express his emotions, then this behaviour is probably present in you. Your parents' approach to money, their attitude towards health and fitness and how they related to each other will have shaped what's important to you in life. Most of the time you're in blissful ignorance about how you are behaving because it's become such an integral part of you over the years. But, every now and then, a stressful situation or a shock triggers an emotional response that appears to be childish or childlike. This is because under stress your deeply programmed behaviours from childhood rise to the surface.

Changing behaviour is hard work

You're reading this book, which indicates that there is a desire to change some aspect of your own behaviour. But it takes lots of effort to change behaviour! You now know consciously that most of your behaviours have been programmed into your unconscious mind. Your conscious and unconscious minds learn in very different ways. Your conscious mind learns through repetition. Can you remember how you learned your times tables at school? I remember having to chant them aloud with the rest of the class over and over again. If you asked me "What's 9 x 8?" I can give you the correct answer without thinking because my times tables were etched into my brain as a child. But they took hours of repetition to learn. Your unconscious mind, however, is like a sponge and absorbs information easily and in vast amounts. This is why children are such quick learners during their first six to seven years. To create a quick and sustainable change to an unwanted behaviour requires you to involve the same mind that learned that behaviour in the first instance. This is usually your unconscious mind.

You can access your unconscious mind through self-hypnosis. When my daughter Rosie was 15, she changed schools in the final year of taking her GCSEs. Her old school was great, but it wasn't a good fit for Rosie, who was deeply unhappy there. Her mock exam results did not reflect the results that she believed she was capable of achieving. She had very little time left to study and revise. One of the subjects she struggled with was French. She started listening to a subliminal hypnosis audio programme every night while she slept. We had no idea as to whether or not it was working until we received her GCSE results. She received a B for French that was a big improvement on the D she had received during her mocks. I was so impressed with the speed of her learning and retention using this unusual method that I developed 30 hypno-meditations that create change whilst you sleep or relax. I've also integrated this hypnotic process into Breathing Space to rewire old and unwanted negative behavioural programmes, without effort!

Unprocessed emotions are toxic

Your emotions are an internal compass that continually provides you with feedback based on whether you are thinking or doing something that is in alignment with your best self or not. Emotions become problematic when they become stuck, trapped, frozen. If you don't express an emotion as it arises within you, choosing instead to push it down for fear of embarrassing yourself, you build an internal volcano of that buried emotion that creates imbalance in your mind and body. Then, when you are least expecting it, something triggers that volcano and you erupt without warning. Your emotional response is totally out of proportion to what is actually going on. There is usually an explanation for why you hold on to old emotions and this typically goes back to your childhood programming. For most people this *explanation* is not accessible because it is buried within their unconscious mind. Then a rather poisonous loop begins: you experience a strong and untethered emotional response and then feel confused about why you reacted so strongly. Your emotional over-reaction doesn't make sense. You ascribe blame to someone, maybe yourself or something that has happened in your environment. You can't be triggered by anyone or anything unless you have these emotions within you in the first place.

My late father was a good and kind man. But on occasions he was full of anger. He would shout at the nightly news, lose his temper if my mum hadn't tidied up after herself and raise his voice to control a conversation. He got an ASBO at the age of 80 for shouting in his local Pizza Express! His anger started aged 11 when he heard about the death of his older brother, who was a flight navigator in World War Two. The shock of losing someone he hero-worshipped and the combination of his austere family environment, where his parents did not express emotion, caused him to suppress his grief. If my dad had been allowed to express his emotions in the moment, he wouldn't have created such a mountain of negativity within him. For years I too had a burning rage within me that used to explode occasionally. Mostly I would take it out on myself and find ways to attack and hurt my body.

Are you poisoning your behavioural roots?

If you consciously suppress, or don't express, emotion you are probably running a programme such as *I can control my emotions* or *It's not safe to say how I feel.* If you unconsciously repress emotions, then your behavioural programme might be *I can't feel anything so I must be okay,* or *It hurts to feel so I choose not to.* In all instances, these ways of holding on to unprocessed emotion are usually caused by an underlying fear. When you watch animals in the wild, they shake after they have escaped from a predator to help them release the extra adrenaline and cortisol caused by fear. Afterwards they relax and return to enjoying the current moment. As a young child you probably had the odd tantrum that released your emotions and you probably felt so much better afterwards.

As an adult, how are you currently releasing pent-up emotions? Most likely you're holding on to many more negative emotions than you realise. Your mind and body are like a garden where trees, plants and flowers flourish when they are cared for and looked after regularly. If you neglect tending to your garden, rampant weeds choke everything else in it. Ultimately, the beautiful emotional landscape you naturally possess becomes obscured by negative emotions that have taken root in every behaviour. Any process that allows you to regularly release your suppressed and repressed emotions is vital to your mental health and wellbeing. Having studied and used many releasing techniques over the years, I integrated a primal releasing process into Breathing Space. You already have an abundance of love and happiness within you – it's simply blocked by unwanted negative emotions that no longer serve you.

The ego and the little white mouse

A few years ago, it was approaching midnight when I was driving home and a light fog had descended upon the roads of Kent. I felt an eerie silence inside the car as I concentrated on driving. As I approached a roundabout, caught in the full beam of my headlights, a little white mouse hurried across the road. It was an extraordinary sight. I was reminded of the time in Portugal when I was training to be a fire-walking instructor. In those days my determination unleashed a testosterone effect within me. I loved a challenge and the tougher it was the better. I had become fixated by learning how to walk on burning coals. I believed that there was a certain trick to doing this and had complete faith that I would master this skill. The instructor said: "Before you walk on the fire, if you think you will get burned, don't walk, because I have no idea how it actually works."

Really?!!!

I couldn't believe what he had just said, yet in true 'Old Nikki' style I launched myself onto the fire whilst frantically screaming "cold moss, cold moss". As the week progressed, the fire-walking challenges got more intense and my feet resembled monstrous blocks of concrete covered in bubble wrap. About halfway through the training we were asked to meditate and connect with our spirit animal. In those days I wasn't spiritually aware and the idea that we have a spirit animal seemed bizarre. As I listened to the sound of soft drumming, a little white mouse dressed as Stuart Little (do you remember the film about a family who adopted a little white mouse?) entered my mind. We were asked to paint our faces in the style of our spirit animal and make animal sounds whilst dancing on the fire. With my face painted white and adorned with black whiskers, I danced on the fire making squeaking sounds. I was conscious that the other participants who had not suffered from a single burn had much grander spirit animals: lions, eagles, stallions and elephants. Here I was, channelling my inner mouse. My egoic mind desperately wanted my spirit animal to be powerful, strong and impressive. My 'inner mouse' made me feel that somehow this was a reflection of my own potential.

You are not your ego

Over the years there have been moments when I've looked up at the twinkling star-scape and felt tiny and insignificant. My ego saw everyone else as better than me, bigger than me, smarter than me, prettier than me, more successful than me. It was a time in my life when I continually compared myself to others. I felt isolated rather than connected to everyone and everything. My ego was a rampaging control freak, and this 'freak' may live within your mind too. It glories in omnipotence. It loves to hold its power over you and uses fear to control. Whenever you feel scared, you are operating from a place of ego rather than from the real you. BUT – you are not your ego.

Everything is connected

You and I are connected to everyone and everything in this vibrant universe. Every thought that you have reverberates across a web of pulsating energy that holds everything and everyone together. The flapping of a butterfly's wings on one side of the world can create a hurricane on the other side of the world. (Chaos theory, or the 'butterfly effect' coined by Edward Lorenz.) Most wars, political and religious issues that are created within this world are caused because there is a tendency to see others as different. And different is judged in some cases as unacceptable. "Is my political party better than your political party?" "Is my god more powerful than your god?" "The colour of my skin is the right colour and that makes the colour of your skin the wrong colour." Are your beliefs misguided because you don't agree with mine? Is my pathway in life the right way? Of course not. These harmful illusions create walls that divide us from each other. What we don't understand we ridicule because we fear it. We stop taking risks in love for fear of looking foolish. We make ourselves walk the path of the masses believing that it must be right for us because everyone else is on that path. We acquire possessions, qualifications, achievements, conquests, relationships to show ourselves how great we really are. Yet these only bring a temporary solace of pleasure when they are motivated from the ego.

Gratitude

When you are grateful for everything that happens to you, both good and bad, then you support your equilibrium to move with greater ease through the natural flow of life. When you stop being grateful, you start to take life for granted. When you listen to your heart you become more aware of the truth about who you really are and what is really important. Most of us are focused most of the time on things that do not really matter. Yet if you were to take a few moments each day to focus on what does, you would enrich your life forever.

The limitation of self-loathing

When you look in a mirror, do you love who you see? Can you love your irritating mannerisms in the same way that you love your courage or your determination? If, like most people, you struggle with the very notion of loving yourself, then you instantly block your ability to feel happy. You may judge yourself harshly for your actions or for your inactions. You may blame yourself when you didn't get the result you wanted. You might feel ashamed of the way you look or something that you did in your past. These perceptions will make you incredibly hard to live with, and you do actually live with yourself all of the time. If you don't love, like, respect and accept who you are, just as you are, then unfortunately you'll never experience anything other than fleeting and illusory happiness. People who suffer from low self-worth want to feel better but don't know how. When you think about alcoholics, drug addicts, compulsive eaters, gamers and other addictive types, they are all wanting to avoid pain and escape from their suffering. For a few moments the illusion of paradise is experienced, a moment's respite in the arid desert they have come to know as life. But you don't need to look outside of yourself to find paradise because it lives brightly within you. It has never left you at any point in your life. But the key to finding it, feeling it, becoming it, requires you to love and accept who you are.

The most important relationship of all

The relationship you have with yourself is the most important relationship you will ever experience. You may think that the state of your happiness is dependent on your partner but that's such a lot of responsibility to put on anyone's shoulders. "You know that I love you and you make me very happy. Without you I can't be happy" – is this emotional blackmail? How you feel is YOUR responsibility and yours alone. I remember hearing the phrase "You complete me" in the *Jerry Maguire* movie, suggesting that completeness will only occur with someone else. What pressure to put on someone! What a pressure to put on yourself! You are enough just as you are. You are already complete just as you are. When you can fall in love with yourself, you create a strong foundation of love within your life. Without love for who you are, how can you truly love anyone or anything else? The more love you feel and share, the more love you'll experience.

What's wrong?

According to psychologist Barbara Fredrickson, positive emotions evolved because they gave your ancestors a good chance of survival. They helped to build communities. In the very early stages of your evolution, the earth was a hostile environment. There were threats from each other, predators, lack of food and water, harsh weather conditions and accidents, because health and safety had not been invented then! To survive you needed to be highly aware and tuned into danger, and your ancestors developed a primal way of perceiving everything through the frame of *What's wrong?* rather than *What's right?* This was a life-saving default programme 300,000 years ago and is still a natural default programme within you today. Have you noticed that the majority of people have a natural tendency to look for what's wrong in a situation or a person, or what's missing from a situation or a person? This behavioural programme is so instinctive that it's hard to notice when we are running it.

Taking off your rose-tinted glasses

The way you perceive anything will determine how you feel. Think about the stages of a relationship. Initially you look at each other through rose-tinted glasses, searching for what's right or wonderful about the person you are attracted to. You find their *unusual habits* utterly charming and cute. As your relationship evolves you both start to relax as you become more comfortable with each other. Without realising it, you have taken off your rose-tinted glasses and started noticing *what's wrong* about that person. Suddenly you're irritated by those charming little habits. The other person hasn't changed – it's your perspective. Because this default perception is unconscious, you need a tangible way of knowing when it is active within you. You have this already in the form of emotions. If you feel a negative emotion when you perceive people or situations, allow yourself to change your perspective by asking yourself questions like: "What's good about this situation?", "What's working well in my relationship?", "What do I love about this person?", "What are the positive insights I've gained from this experience?" and "How have I grown as a result of this difficulty?" The more you guide your perceptions by paying attention to how you feel means that you gradually align yourself to happiness.

Put on your silver boots again!

Five years ago, just before Christmas, I was watching my mum, who was wired up with tubes and on a ventilator in the intensive care unit. I was amazed by her fighting spirit. When the will to live is strong within you and you have a strong purpose for survival, then you are physically strengthened. My mum's purpose was a pair of ludicrously high silver boots that she was desperate to wear on Christmas Day! Mum has always been a creative and eccentric maverick. As a child I remember her sliding down the stair rail wearing a red negligee singing Shirley Bassey's iconic number 'Big Spender'. My younger brother, sister and I would be sitting around the table eating our Weetabix and my mum would jump on the table and finish off her routine with a flourish. It was only when we started going to friends' houses for sleepovers that we realised this was not how mothers usually behaved!

I remember that mum used to sell antiques at Greenwich Market wearing her patchwork circular skirts and shoelaces tied around her head. She was passionate about postcards, old books and her dogs – "I find dogs so much easier than people." Growing up I would feel excruciatingly embarrassed by my mum's behaviour at times, yet she was a big hit with my friends, who would open up to her about all their own problems. The years have not dulled her penchant for glamorous clothes and even though she is in her eighties she still wears PVC leggings and flouncy tops that float higher than a butterfly on acid.

With Christmas approaching, my mum had already planned her outfit for the big day. A silver top with white leggings and the pièce de résistance – a pair of silver stiletto boots! She calls them her 'gin and tonic' boots; she can't actually walk in them, but they do look fabulous. Those boots became a symbol for motivating her to heal and recover: "Mum, we need to see you in those silver boots!" Whether or not my mum could hear what we were saying, every time we visited her in hospital, we kept on talking about her boots. Whilst a tiny part of me was faintly appalled that my mother would wear such outrageous clothes, another part of me, the louder part of me, felt thrilled that she was refusing to grow old gracefully. Her silver boots taught me the valuable lesson that if it feels good, then do it! Life is for living.

Are you caught up in people-pleasing?

Are you experiencing thrills from silver boots? When you relinquish your inhibitions about looking foolish or different, you liberate yourself and have so much more fun. But do you worry about what people think of you? Do you fear being judged and get anxious when you don't fit in? Are you afraid of looking like a fool? You may find yourself so caught up in *people-pleasing* that you forget to please yourself. You say "yes" when you really want to say "no". Have you forgotten how to fully embrace and enjoy life?

Enjoying the moment

Sometimes when you least expect it, something remarkable dries the tears in your eyes. You notice something gleaming in the greyness. A shiny glinting hint of naughtiness that shouts to the world, "Let's laugh for a while!" You feel an inner conviction, an innate courage that motivates you to step out and step up with a boldness. Your pulse quickens and your heart begins to thump with the exhilaration of the freedom of being true to yourself. These moments are your way of wearing your own pair of silver boots. As the world appears to conspire to perpetuate insanity, mindless violence, suffering and death, the spirit of your silver boots continues to shine. They represent hope and optimism that no matter how dark life appears, how tough the struggle of your existence, you can still find something to believe in, something that uplifts you, higher than the highest heel. Whatever you're caught up in now, I urge you to take a deep breath and look around you. Somewhere in your life you will see them, a shiny symbol that causes your heart to sing and fills your belly with the resounding vibration of laughter.

Removing your blocks

Understanding the different blocks to your happiness is an important step to understanding why you feel so stressed. But awareness of these blocks is not enough to create a rapid change in how you feel. When I created Breathing Space I wanted to ensure that the technique would work relentlessly by chipping away the blocks until you are liberated into freedom from pain and stress. Breathing Space works but it doesn't work without your commitment. You don't go to the gym for one week and think, "That's it now, I've got a healthy body for the rest of my life." The more you practise Breathing Space, the more blocks you'll clear and neutralise. Imagine a brick wall. There are many bricks in that wall. First you have to find a way to loosen the bricks because they are held together with strong cement. Sometimes you can knock a huge hole in your wall and you can remove several bricks at once. At other times it takes patience and diligence to remove just one brick. Hold in mind that to be the best version of who you are requires making yourself a promise. A promise that you will carve out a little bit of time every day dedicated to clearing away your unwanted and unprocessed blocks. This means that when something happens in the present moment, you are better equipped to deal with it.

4

ARE YOU SURVIVING OR THRIVING?

As a human being, you naturally search for a sense of order, coherence, continuity and justice. Psychologist Abraham Maslow's well-known hierarchy of needs diagram demonstrates that until you feel safe and secure, it becomes harder to grow and develop strong, connected relationships. As you experience life and all of its challenges, you have developed coping mechanisms designed to protect you and keep you safe. Not just physically but emotionally too.

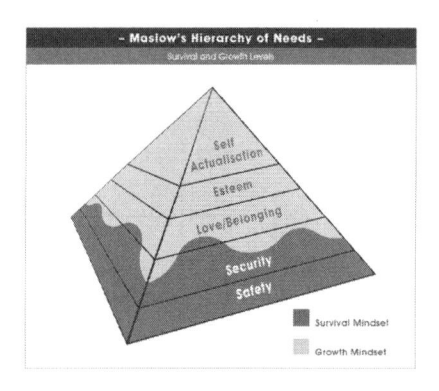

A cellular reaction

The ability to feel safe and to create a place of safety is helped by understanding what happens to you at a cellular level. 'You' are a community of something like 50 trillion cells. Each one has a membrane that surrounds the cell and allows nutrients to enter it. In the centre is the nucleus that contains genetic information.

Before the brilliant breakthrough of epigenetics, traditional cellular biologists believed in *genetic determinism*. This came from the premise that you don't choose the genes that you're born with and your genes control your life. But what if your genes predispose you to physical and emotional issues? Is the only answer a visit to an allopathic medical practitioner who will often treat the symptoms rather than the cause? This theory of *genetic determinism* places you as a victim within your own life and is, in my view, so last century. Following research on cloning stem cells over 50 years ago, cellular biologist Bruce Lipton discovered that the nucleus of the cell doesn't do anything unless it receives signals from the receptors on the cell's membrane. He discovered that approximately 90% of genes are continually responding to signals from your inner and outer environment.

A cellular lockdown

Your cells have two operating mechanisms. When you feel calm and full of energy, your body releases serotonin and oxytocin. With this your cells' receptors sense that the environment is safe, which causes an opening up of how your cells respond. The chemistry in your body is now growing and thriving. Conversely, if you feel stressed or anxious you start releasing cortisol, adrenaline and norephedrine. Your cells' receptors sense danger and feel threatened by the toxicity of these hormones and respond to a primal need to protect themselves by closing down and effectively hibernating. Your cells are operating from a survival function. The genes involved with immune system health have shut down, compromising your immune system. When your immune system has been weakened, this can lead to immunodeficiency disorders that prevent your body from being able to fight off infections and diseases.

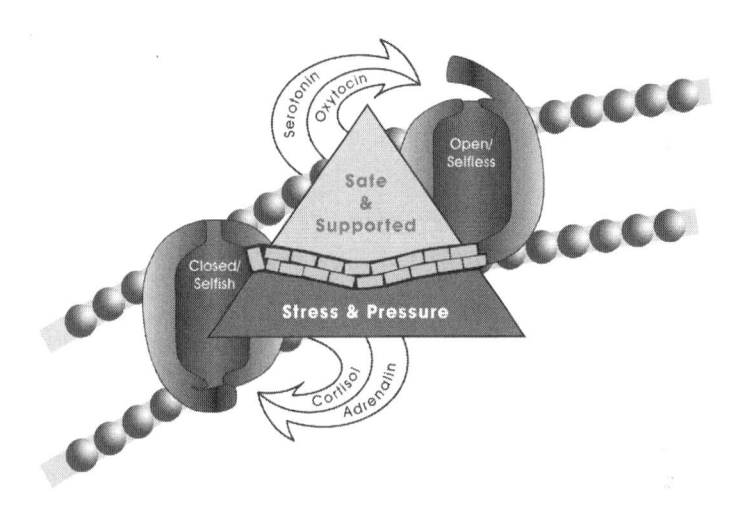

Covid-19 and fear

As a little girl one of my favourite toys was a snow globe. The miniature village inside was continually changing because every time I shook it, the swirling snow would always settle in a different way. At the beginning of 2020, Planet Earth was shaken up dramatically by Covid-19. This invisible and omnipotent virus created an immediate and profound change in the behaviour of most people. The panic and fear of death was fuelled by the media, who shared graphic images, and gave frightening accounts and news reports of the reasons why people around the world should feel scared. Many of the population experienced fear so intense that they existed in a state of overwhelm, unable to think, unable to move as every cough fuelled the belief that they too may have *got it*. Many people felt extremely worried about money, food shortages, mortgage repayments and the safety of loved ones. Images of hospitals and people on ventilators, video diaries from overworked doctors and stories of conspiracy theories created a terror that was palpable by many. People who had saved hard all their lives watched helplessly as their savings and investments disappeared. Brave individuals who provided vital services, such as supermarket staff and medical teams, knowingly placed themselves at risk every time they showed up for work. Panic buyers whose trolleys were laden with toilet rolls and pasta stormed past bewildered elderly people who stared helplessly at the empty shelves. People whose livelihoods were destroyed in days, small businesses that were started with great hope and optimism and even people who others may have perceived as 'sitting pretty' felt broken as economic markets plunged in the face of an unprecedented global crisis.

Fear attacks your immune system

Then something rather unusual happened in the spring of 2020. Reports started appearing about the growing numbers of inexplicable *extra* deaths that could not be attributed to Covid-19. Could it be that for many people around the world, their fear levels had reached an overwhelming intensity and at this point their immune systems would have been compromised? Fear lowers your immune system, stops you from thinking clearly and creates a resistance to anything positive. Fear gathers momentum quickly, like an express train building up speed. There comes a point when the momentum of fear is so great that it's almost impossible to stop feeling it. Any decisions you make when you're feeling scared are often totally different to the decisions you make when you're feeling safe and calm. Your behaviour changes under stressful conditions and people often describe this phenomenon as "I don't feel like me any more".

The placebo and nocebo effects

Pharmaceutical companies factor the placebo effect into their clinical trials. It is a phenomenon based on the premise that if you believe something will have a positive impact on you, then it usually does. There are numerous documented cases of people who reversed cancer, or recovered from heart disease, depression and crippling arthritis, by believing in a placebo. Similarly, there are numerous cases of how others have become sick and even died after being misdiagnosed with a fatal illness. This is known as the nocebo effect – when you believe that something will have a negative effect on you, then it usually does. Negative emotions trigger the 50 trillion cells in your body to close down and depress your immune system. Your emotional and physical self is intertwined to such an extent that the way you choose to view your external world affects your mental and emotional health. Belief can be so strong that pharmaceutical companies integrate double-blind randomised studies when evaluating new drugs, to try to remove the power of the mind over the body.

The Big Apple Experiment

Understanding the impact that thoughts and emotions are having on your body's chemistry, immune system and mindset is hard to relate to with diagrams of cells alone. I wanted to create an experiment that would bring cellular biology to life. I was driven by the need to find a way of demonstrating how individuals are unconsciously hurting or healing themselves.

Photo taken by Nelis van Veen, a 12-year-old Dutch boy who did his own apple experiment.

In 2009 I introduced the Big Apple Experiment to show the impact of thoughts on physical reality. It caused lots of controversy when a double page spread appeared in the *Daily Mail*, 'Can talking to apples make you beautiful?' I chose to work with apples because they contain about 65% water, a similar percentage of water to that which an average adult has in their body. You place half an apple into a jar labelled LOVE and the other half into a jar labelled FEAR. For two to three weeks you imagine sending these two different emotions into your respective apple halves. The majority of people who choose to do this experiment see a visible change between the rates of decay between each apple half. Your emotional mood *is* contagious and depending upon whether you're feeling positive or negative emotions, you are continually impacting upon your health.

Impact of stress on genetically identical twins

There are examples of twins who are genetically identical yet one twin experienced more stress and therefore this created a marked difference between the appearance within each set of twins. Increased stress in one twin caused weight gain, alopecia (spontaneously occurring hair loss) and ageing.

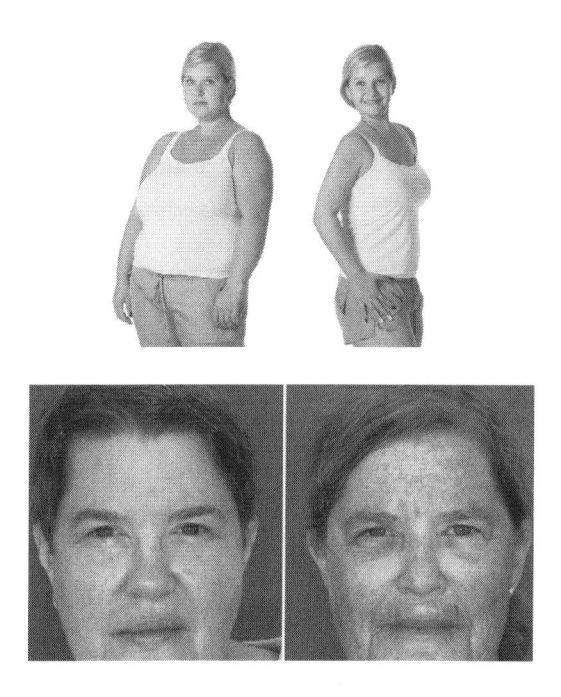

Your body is a natural healer

The power that made your body, heals your body. When your mind and body are functioning properly, then your body naturally heals, repairs and restores itself. Mental and physical health challenges occur when you experience negative emotions on a frequent basis. These emotions add stress within your body and hamstring your natural healing capability. Breathing Space reconnects you to your body's innate ability to heal and repair.

Brainwave patterns

Your brain is made up of billions of brain cells called neurons, that use electricity to communicate with each other. The combination of millions of neurons sending and receiving signals produces an enormous amount of electrical activity in the brain. These signals are detected using sensitive medical equipment (such as an EEG), to measure electrical levels. These are brainwave patterns and have a cyclic, wave-like nature. The rate per second (frequency) of these patterns changes based on what you are doing and how you are feeling.

Brainwave frequencies

Beta frequencies have a range of 16–31 Hz and are emitted when you are alert, agitated, tense or afraid. **Alpha** frequencies have a range of 8–15 Hz and are emitted when you are physically and mentally relaxed. **Theta** frequencies have a range of 4–7 Hz and are emitted when meditating or experiencing a deep trance. This theta frequency creates the perfect conditions within your mind and body to heal and repair. **Delta** frequencies have a range of 0.1–3 Hz and are emitted when you are fast asleep. According to neuroscientists, who actively research the link between brain frequencies and health, slowing down the frequency of your brainwave patterns increases levels of neurotransmitters such as endorphins and dopamine that make you feel good.

Linking cellular function with brainwave frequencies

Your cells have a nervous system and their cellular function is affected by your brainwave frequencies. A beta frequency causes cells to close down and operate in survival mode. A theta frequency causes cells to open up into growth mode. Stress is compounded by your cellular function and brainwave frequency. If you change just one of those elements – stress, cellular function or brainwave frequency – then you will affect all of them.

Binaural beats

In 1839 the physicist Heinrich Wilhelm Dove discovered a technique to change the frequency of brainwave function. When two pure tones at slightly different frequencies are listened to by your left and right ear at the same time, your brain responds by creating a beat that is called a binaural beat. In 1973 biophysicist Dr Gerald Oster accelerated binaural beat technology in the realisation of their impact on brainwave frequency. If you are someone who struggles to meditate because you're feeling anxious and stressed, your brainwaves will be emitting at a beta frequency. Trying to slow down your brainwave frequency into theta is challenging when you have cortisol and adrenaline in your body. When you listen to binaural beats that emit at a theta frequency, your brainwave frequency naturally aligns to the frequency of the binaural beat.

My own experiment

In 2010 I began testing binaural beat recordings with attendees of open seminars that I delivered for a period of five years at Shakespeare's Globe Theatre, in the Balcony Room. Working with a scientist and an electrical engineer, Hugo Jenks, we decided to test the impact of binaural beat recordings on apples. Working with apples cut into halves, Hugo played different binaural beats to the apple halves labelled 'A' for 30 minutes daily for two weeks and the halves labelled 'B' were left in a different room and were not exposed to binaural beat recordings. The conclusion of the experiment was that exposure to binaural beats that combined alpha and theta frequencies slowed down the rate of decay during this period. The other half of the apple showed a 40% decay level. You can access more information about this experiment and other experiments I did with apples and binaural beats in my book *Charismatic to the Core*, published in 2015.

Breathing Space incorporates a powerful binaural beats sequence designed to gently guide your brainwave frequency into alignment with your body's natural healing ability. As this process occurs, your cells will change their operating function from survival to growth. As you practise Breathing Space, you'll become increasingly aware of your ability to enter a deep meditative state quickly.

5

REALITY IS NOT REAL!

Your external reality is just a perception of what you think your reality to be. Your external reality is a projection of the thoughts, concepts and beliefs you hold, and the emotions that you feel. Your perception of your world is always inaccurate and incomplete because your mind and five senses aren't equipped to process the fullest extent of what really exists outside yourself. If you've ever revisited your infant school as an adult, you may well have been surprised at how tiny everything seemed. Your perceptions change with your life's experience. As you grow, learn and develop, you expand your awareness and this changes your perception, and consequently your attitudes. Ultimately, your perception of what you believe to be real is simply a perception that exists only inside your mind. That's why two people can experience the same situation completely differently. That's why there is no 'right' or 'wrong' perception, just the perception you have in that moment. How you perceive others will consequently inform your judgements about them. Their perception of why they are acting as they are will be different to yours. Just being aware of the illusory aspect of perception helps you to adopt a more accepting and wiser view of people and situations. When you focus on what you don't want, you colour your internal perception accordingly. You unwittingly look for examples to validate why you are unhappy, and you will always find those examples! You only see what you are looking for.

Your human senses

Your five physical senses and your mind/awareness are the way you process information about your external world. They are referred to as *senses* because they are how you make *sense* of what is outside of you. Although your senses have a great range of sensitivity, they are, in comparison to other species, somewhat limited. A dog can hear the sound of a high-pitched whistle that you won't be able to hear because their hearing range is approximately twice as wide compared to a human's. You may have heard the expression 'having an eagle eye'. This is because birds of prey have eyesight estimated as being four to eight times stronger than that of the average human. Bears can smell something from 20 miles away because the olfactory bulb region in their brain is five times larger than in a human brain. Catfish have approximately 175,000 taste buds located all over their bodies compared to the 10,000 tiny taste buds that you have. A jewel beetle (a tiny insect) can sense a fire from a distance of 50 miles away. Your human senses are constricting your awareness and are continually influencing your perceptions.

Sensory overwhelm damages your wellbeing

The deeper your awareness, the more likely you are to optimise your experiences during your life. If your senses are overstimulated, they become anaesthetised. They lose their sensitivity and obscure your perceptions, as if you are covering the world with a layer of thick dust. It's like getting into your car with a dirty windscreen – you're unaware of this obscuration until you switch on your windscreen wipers, then the entire world looks brighter!

Today's busy world is full of stimuli, crammed with opportunities for sensory overwhelm. I've never been able to enjoy live concerts because the loud pulsating sounds affect my nervous system, causing my body to shut down. Your senses will be continually adapting and trying to process the variety and level of sensory stimuli around you. This is why stress is such a growing problem. Technology has taken sensory overload to a whole new level. The average person checks their smartphone every 12 minutes and growing numbers of people are becoming addicted to this high level of cognitive and emotional stimulation. Checking your smartphone before bedtime creates a number of effects that prevent you from sleeping well. The blue light that your smartphone emits is bad for your vision and suppresses your melatonin levels, which is the hormone responsible for controlling your sleep-wake cycle. Information overload short-circuits your nervous system; thinking and reasoning become dulled; decision-making is flawed and, in some cases, impossible. Research carried out by Dr Glenn Wilson at the London Institute of Psychiatry found that persistent distractions create a ten-point fall in IQ. Eventually this leads to physical and emotional disturbances. In his book *Future Shock*, Alvin Toffler referred to this phenomenon as 'Future Shock Syndrome'. Your mind's attention is continually being activated, causing distraction of your attention. It becomes difficult to stick to one task and you become habituated to thinking and processing information at speed. If you're a driver, then you've probably driven many times on a motorway. The experience of driving in the inside lane at 60mph is completely different to overtaking at 80mph in the outside lane. The difference in speed creates additional tension. When driving at a safe speed you'll probably be using your *peripheral* vision – this gives you an expanded awareness of what's happening around you as well as in front of you. When you become tense, you use your foveal vision when you focus on what is directly in front of you. Your overall awareness contracts, your body tenses with the release of cortisol and your breathing becomes shallow. Your driving capability will have become impaired and you probably don't notice this response. If you are living your life at this pace, your cellular function will be operating in survival mode, your brainwave frequency will be in beta and your body can't heal and feel well when it's placed under these conditions.

Expanded awareness requires single-focused attention

In 1975 Hungarian-American psychologist, Professor Mihály Csíkszentmihályi identified a high-performing state of awareness that he referred to as a 'flow state'. In the world of sport, you probably hear of this state described as 'being in the zone'. When you are fully immersed in something that you enjoy, you acquire an energised focus and possess greater clarity of awareness. To access this expanding state, you find a way to ignore the external distractions, slow down your thoughts and maintain a steady focus on one thing, for example your breath or a candle flame. As you practise this quiet concentration, you'll feel as if your mind and body have undertaken a rigorous emotional and physical detox – a cleansing respite contained in the silence of a few minutes. After years of excess information cluttering and blocking your nervous system, you'll feel peaceful, balanced and calm. With equanimity you'll perform better, your decision-making faculty improves, and you feel more connected with others. Ultimately your awareness of what is truly important for you expands and gives you crystal-clear clarity.

Sifting and sorting information

Since Galen, a Greek physician $c.$AD 130–200, recognised the possibility of the unconscious mind, there have been hundreds of philosophers, contemplatives, psychologists and neuroscientists who have identified the vast streams of information, (estimates range from two to ten million bits of information) which flow into the unconscious mind from the physical senses. In his book *The Biology of Belief*, Dr Bruce Lipton claims that the conscious mind can only process 40 bits of information every second, yet your unconscious mind brings in 500,000 times more than this! Your unconscious mind is like a bubbling cauldron of thoughts and behavioural programmes, many of which don't make it into your conscious awareness.

Your childhood beliefs

Your beliefs are a collection of habitual thoughts. They shape your perceptions and have a huge impact on your behaviour. Imagine as a young child coming home from school, feeling excited because you scored nine out of ten in your spelling test. Your mum might have asked you about the word you got wrong. This may have created a belief "I'm not good enough!" or "I need to be perfect for Mummy to love me". Even if your mum was only trying to help you, her focus on the one word that you got wrong holds the potential to create a belief that limits you throughout your life.

It's amazing to witness how a belief formed as a very young child has been kept alive throughout someone's life. I helped an IT director who had a heart attack at age 44 and he was terrified of having another one. We tracked his unconscious fear back to a memory when he was six years old. He and his friends had decided that whatever the number of the house they currently lived in was, that would be the age when they would die. He was living at house number 44, and his unconscious mind manifested this childhood belief.

Your emotional guidance system

How do you make decisions? Over the years I've worked with people who were experiencing problems within their relationships. They present me with a list of the pros and cons of staying with their partner. The problem with trying to make *logical decisions* is that if any decision you make doesn't feel good, then you'll unconsciously sabotage that decision. You have an internal guidance system that you've probably not been optimising! This guidance system, formed from the emotions you feel, advises you about whether you are living your life in or out of alignment with your best self. Every emotion you experience is impermanent. It will appear, disappear, increase and decrease its intensity and sometimes morph into a completely different emotion entirely. When you watch a movie, the emotions you experience are based on your perception of that movie. Although you experience different emotional responses, at some level you know that it is just a movie. Well, your life is a movie of your own perceptions. When you understand that your thoughts are not YOU, your emotions are not YOU, everything feels different inside. Often something in your external world can trigger an emotional memory from your past. For example, one of your friends might say something that reminds you of a strict teacher from school who frightened you as a child. You're not just responding to what your friend is saying; you're also responding to underlying fears.

Don't judge your emotions too harshly

Do you have a tendency to label your emotions as positive or negative? If you judge your emotional responses, you are telling yourself "It's not safe to feel". If you view 'negative' emotions as feedback, this offers a more constructive view about them. If you try to ignore negative emotions, these pesky little fellows wriggle through their escape route to the surface and will build in their level of intensity. Pushing them down only makes them more tenacious! All emotions come from a place of love and are your friends. It is the unprocessed emotions held in the mind/body that create imbalance. The next time you visit a supermarket, notice how young children respond when one of their parents tells them that they can't have any sweets. Most kids will rage and pummel their fists and stamp their feet. If they are ignored by their parent, you'll witness that their rage intensifies as it rises to the surface then releases quickly. Then the child becomes calm and behaves normally. Children naturally use this primal way of releasing emotions. Sadly, at some point in your life you stopped practising primal releasing. Instead of liberating your negative emotions, you may have pushed them down into your unconscious mind. Whilst you might not feel their presence on a day-to-day basis, these suppressed or repressed emotions will be affecting your cellular function and your brainwave frequencies.

Don't bury your negative emotions

Negative emotions left to fester will create a limescale residue that builds a stronger wall around the heart. You'll have heard the expression 'they've hardened their heart'. This isn't just an abstract metaphor to describe emotional blockages. The heart responds to increased stress caused by chronically raised blood pressure by thickening its muscle wall. If over the years you experience too much pain, your heart wall hardens like a buttress, causing you to feel disconnected and isolated. During the work I've done with clients over the years, they report afterwards that they feel *a strange, growing sensation in their heart.* This is the physical expression of the heart's response to the release of emotional pain. Psychotherapists now unanimously agree that your psyche (which is not YOU but an expression of you) can be likened to an iceberg. It's easy to focus on the tip that remains visible above the surface. You might put on a brave face, smile when you're feeling upset, take action when you're feeling scared. Underneath the surface of your 'waterline' there is an iceberg of frozen emotions. Before you can release negative emotions, the ice needs to thaw so the trapped emotions can flow.

Primal releasing liberates you

If you don't do anything to release your trapped emotions, they begin to scream about the injustice of it. It gets harder to maintain a sense of control and, in doing so, creates a disconnection from other people. The smallest thing can trigger buried emotions that, without warning, explode up onto the surface, causing tremors of fear throughout your body. Holding on to negative emotions in the mind/body is draining. When you feel safe you *express* your emotions; when you feel fearful, then you push them down consciously or unconsciously. Many of the challenges that you experience within your life now are due to the emotions that you didn't feel safe to process and express. Holding on to old negative emotions about anything creates an internal battle that's exhausting. Stop the battle with your own buried emotions because they burden you in every context of your life.

Opening up a can of worms

Breathing Space includes primal releasing so you can liberate yourself regularly from the constraints of negative emotions. You can do this without having to do a painful review of past traumas because it's a physical releasing process. Not everyone wants to open a can of worms, because there is a belief that it is then impossible to put the lid back on again. With primal releasing you don't just open the can; you clear out every single worm so that the lid no longer serves a purpose.

Attachment to being a victim

There is something strangely addictive about moaning, blaming and ascribing the reason for your unhappiness onto someone or something else. You may believe that if your life was less challenging, you'd feel happier. If your family was more reliable, you'd feel less stressed. If your children were more obedient, life would be calmer! It's so easy to operate from the premise that other people, things or situations are the reason for why you don't feel happy. It's incredibly stressful and takes huge amounts of effort and energy to change anyone or anything other than yourself. It feels like swimming against the ocean's tide. You'll eventually become so exhausted with the continual struggle that you'll either go with the natural flow of the tide or drown in the ocean.

The need to fix others

Rather than accepting people just as they are, you may feel the urge or impulse to 'fix' them. No one is broken and nothing needs fixing. It's just that the way you are perceiving these aspects of your life is not helpful. Other people don't change unless they want to. When you change the way that you look at people, they often appear to change as if some miracle has occurred overnight. You created that miracle when you changed how you saw them. The late Wayne Dyer, one of my favourite motivational teachers, said, "Change the way you look at things and the things you look at change."

This insight gives you so much power. You have all the resources within you to transform every perception of anyone or anything that doesn't make you feel uplifted.

Releasing negative emotions changes your perspective

If you're feeling stressed, then this will skew your perspective. Everything around you will be observed through a lens of stress. When you look at the world through the eyes of love and compassion, everyone and everything appears to be different. Two of my favourite questions when people are experiencing challenges are "What would love say to this person?" and "What would love do in this situation?". These questions create an emotional shift that changes people's perspective. Holding on to negative emotions creates a different life experience in contrast to someone who is prepared to continually let go of their old and unprocessed emotions.

Love is the ultimate shape-shifter

The more stress you release, the more you realise that you have so much love within you. This awareness of the love within you is projected into your reality. Do you remember the first time you fell in love? You saw the whole world as a wonderful, magical place. You became more tolerant, more loving, more generous. Love expands and builds strong connections with others. Stress is fear. If you think about situations and people that trigger stress in you, what are you afraid of? Fear diminishes and shrivels who you are. Fear keeps you small in the shadows of pettiness. Fear causes you to move from selflessness into selfishness and you care less about others. Fear suppresses your immunology and closes down your cells. You can't fight fear with fear because it simply intensifies your awareness of fear. You can't find peace by punishing others who have hurt you. Your continued growth and expansion will only happen when you are driven by love rather than fear. Love is stronger than any other emotion because it is fundamentally who you are. When you make decisions from a place of fear, you contaminate your life because you're acting in a way that is totally disregarding who you are.

When parents use threats to get their children to conform, just like I did with my own daughter for a time, both the parent and child feel diminished because their true essence is being disregarded. When leaders try to improve productivity by control and ruthless behaviour, they drain the spirit of their workforce as well as their own. When your need to win dominates the pleasure you get from a sport that you play, then that pleasure becomes conditional on winning rather than experiencing. When you criticise yourself or others for any reason, then you block your connection to the infinite source of love that is your true nature.

The Tree of Compassion

© 2019 The Tree of Compassion Model is subject to copyright and is owned by Nikki J Owen Limited

Imagine a large tree with roots that grow deep into the soil. The quality of the soil will nourish the growth of branches that stretch and expand into the sky. When the soil and climate are in alignment with the tree's needs, then fruit will ripen and grow plump with juicy sweetness. Once the fruit has grown into ripeness, it is ready to be picked. If it's left for too long it begins to decay and eventually falls onto the ground, reintegrating back into the soil that nourished its creation. Everything is impermanent. Every phase of the tree's existence supports the next phase in its evolution. If the soil becomes contaminated by a toxic substance, then the entire ecosystem of that tree is damaged, sometimes irrevocably. The environment that creates the perfect conditions for you to thrive and grow is love. If you poison your own soil with toxic emotions such as anger, fear, grief or guilt, then you poison the ecosystem of You. The ease with which you might have manifested the fruits of your labour and experienced the sweetness of life will become arduous and unfulfilling. When you can love the poison as much as the sweetness, then you neutralise the toxicity. It is relatively easy to love loveable people and loveable aspects about yourself. It's easy to love a warm sunny day and love the carpet of bluebells in May. Yet true compassion loves regardless, and with the flowering potential of unbridled compassion you discover that it's your natural way to love everything.

Seeing what you expect

A number of years ago I was attending a national conference for the British Society of Dowsers when one of the speakers showed the audience of over a hundred people a video of two teams playing basketball and asked us to count the occasions that one of the teams had possession of the ball. When she showed us the same video again most of the audience, including myself, did not see that as well as the two teams, there was a person dressed in a gorilla costume, walking around on the court! You see what you expect to see and if something occurs that doesn't fit with your expectations then you don't see it. Your brain uses predictive processing to make guided guesses about your external world. Your experiences and your emotional state will influence how you interpret what you perceive. If something occurs that is outside of your expectation, your brain makes the adjustments and amends your perception accordingly. In experiments by French physician Augustin Charpentier in 1891, participants were given a small and a large ball of the same weight. Most people wrongly reported that the large ball was heavier, because in their experience if there are two objects made from the same substance, the larger the object, the heavier it becomes. Your expectations about what you believe you can create in your life will be created by your expectations. Isn't this another example of how the placebo and nocebo effects impact upon the physical expression of your life?

German philosopher Immanuel Kant (1724–1804) said that reality in and of itself is unknowable and subjective. You interpret the information from your senses into something that becomes meaningful to you. For example, a word describing an emotion is just a collection of letters presented in a certain way. Your experience of that word will be unique to you, based on what that word triggers within you. The word 'love' can cause great joy in one individual but heartache in another. The actual word itself is meaningless; it is the personal meaning you have attached to that word that creates your emotional response in that moment. Ultimately the way you perceive *everything* is a choice. Given that you can't ever know what is really happening in the external world, you can choose a way of looking at that world that gives you the best feeling. This choice is your point of power. When I first started delivering masterclasses, I noticed that the participants were very quiet and didn't ask many questions. It would have been easy to form the opinion that they were bored. This was not a helpful way of perceiving their response. If I had allowed my mind to wander down this particular train of thinking, I would have become nervous and tentative. This would have affected my breath, and my voice would have sounded strained. I might have flushed and gone bright red as the mounting panic to please rose up within me. I ascribed a different meaning to their *bored* reaction: "They must be so mesmerised that they can't put into words the impact that my message is having on them." Who knows what they were really thinking, but with my new interpretation, I enjoyed the masterclass! I've learned that what really matters is finding a way of interpreting your perceptions so you feel empowered.

Changing perceptions with love

Your unconscious programmes initiate the same old perceptions – this is not helpful. It is in the realisation of your power to choose your perceptions that you change your awareness. With time you'll realise that you can always look for the positive aspects within people, situations and yourself. You consequently appreciate more of what is good in your life. Breathing Space gently encourages a gentle shift in the way you perceive life, so you feel more at peace with how things are. You'll notice that you become more grateful for what you have.

6

WHO ARE YOU?

To fully appreciate the incredible potential you have, regardless of what's happening to you in your life right now, requires you to understand that the larger aspect of you is pure non-physical awareness. Understanding a little about consciousness explains so much about the meaning and experiences of life. For many years I felt scared and inhibited about sharing my thoughts as a lay person on a subject that was usually reserved for scientists or academics or spiritual contemplatives. As I allowed my own curiosity to lead me into a greater awareness of consciousness, I began seeing that it is the root for understanding those things that appear to be inexplicable. Consciousness allows you to experience who you are and why you're here from an elevated, big picture perspective. Until recently, Western science has preferred to understand more about the objective physical world rather than how it links to the subjective non-physical world of consciousness.

Uncharted territory

When Albert Einstein's work on the unified field theory referred to time and space as illusion, many scientists agreed with his philosophy but didn't know what to do with it. Scientists and academics are making giant leaps forward with the realisation that people are more than physical beings created from matter. In the 1600s when the astronomer Galileo first used a telescope to observe space, he immediately disproved a belief that had been held for centuries, that the sun and planets orbited around the earth. The invention of the telescope created more awareness of planetary behaviour. As people's awareness expands, when they begin to focus their mind in the same way that a telescope focuses on the stars, old beliefs are challenged and changed. Humanity can put human beings on the moon and send space shuttles to Mars. Yet the infinite nature of consciousness still remains uncharted territory for many people.

The world is like unset jelly

Nobel Prize-winning physicists have proven that the world of 'matter' is made from a sea of pulsating particles of energy that flash into and out of being, millisecond after millisecond. Nothing is solid. This is the fascinating subject of quantum mechanics. Your thoughts are electrical impulses that are changing the environment on a particle by particle basis. Nothing in life has inherent existence. Everything needs something else for it to become a physical manifestation within your awareness. Imagine the world as unset jelly. Your attention to a part of that jelly causes that part to set and become real. Nothing exists in your reality until it is drawn into your awareness. This is why what you give your attention to will strengthen what you are giving your attention to. If you focus on a person's negative attributes, you strengthen your awareness of those attributes and it gets harder to notice anything except that which is negative. But if you focus on all the positive attributes of the same individual, then your perception of that individual changes. Your perception does an extremely convincing job of masquerading as reality, but it's not reality you're experiencing, it's a projection of what you've given your attention to. Being human means that your perception of an individual or a situation creates an emotional response. The world is full of upsetting situations and events. There are many people who hurt and damage others. This makes it challenging to maintain a positive feeling. Are you showing a lack of compassion if you are choosing to be unaffected by these things? Not at all. Remember, your continued focus on those people or situations that cause you to feel any negative emotion is damaging you, and this in turn negatively impacts on those people around you.

Nuclear physicist demystifies the 'woo'

Buddhism helped me to gain an understanding of consciousness in a simplistic way. Over the years as a non-scientist, I have worked with thousands of analytical people who rely on scientific research and have labelled some aspects of my work as 'woo'. Trying to explain consciousness was always challenging until I was introduced to Thomas Campbell, a nuclear physicist who has brought together philosophy, physics and metaphysics. He taught me that understanding and acknowledging consciousness is vital for transformation. His electrifying trilogy *My Big TOE* delivers a major scientific breakthrough that demonstrates the unifying field of infinite intelligence and reinforces the importance of recognising that you are mainly non-physical awareness.

Consciousness – a digital information field

Think about your physical body as a computer. Its physical presence started to evolve when you first had the desire that triggered a thought: "I want a computer." It became more real once you'd ordered it online and it arrived in its box. Even when you set it all up, it didn't work until you switched it on. You had to give life to your computer! Then, using Wi-Fi you wanted to connect to a digital information field, much like consciousness, that holds the potential to show you any type of information. Every thought, every idea, every experience is held within this field but as far as you're concerned it doesn't exist. You have to know what you want to search for. You have to have an idea that leads to an intention that drives you to type into Google whatever you want to give your attention to. Then all sorts of choices are presented on your screen. Pages and pages of options. Because there is a huge choice and your time is limited, you probably click on links on the very first page without delving deeper into the awareness of other options. As you search for what you want, your knowledge begins to grow and expand and you're continually informing Google's algorithms – in the same way that your physical senses have created their own set of algorithms that changes your data about reality. At what point does something become real? Did your own reality begin when you became aware of the desire to purchase a computer?

There comes a point in your computer's life cycle that it doesn't function that well. The parts are wearing out and the model you bought five years ago has been improved beyond recognition. You buy another computer, and even though this new computer is totally different and has far superior functioning, you still access exactly the same stuff that you accessed from your old computer. However, your awareness has expanded and grown. You've refined your methods for searching, you've learned how to avoid the distractions of the pop-up ads and you've deepened your understanding of some subjects. Your consciousness is growing and evolving all the time, regardless of how your body is evolving and aging. You are so much more than your physical body. Your awareness can go anywhere, do anything and have any experience that it wants.

What is really real?

My understanding of consciousness and energy was accelerated when I experienced ayahuasca. This plant-based medicine has been used by indigenous people for over four thousand years for the purposes of physical, emotional and spiritual healing. The process itself is unpleasant because the plant extract causes you to purge! Friends of mine raved about Rythmia Life Advancement Centre in Costa Rica, the only medically accredited centre in the world which is licensed to hold ayahuasca ceremonies. I will never forget the bizarre sight that greeted me as I walked into a wooden temple. Eighty mattresses had been arranged closely together. Placed carefully on each one was a blanket, a toilet roll and a bucket! It didn't really reassure me – I just couldn't imagine how awkward it was going to be throwing up next to a stranger. Most ayahuasca ceremonies are held overnight and are treated as sacred rituals. The shaman and his group of helpers opened the ceremony with chanting, stamping and a blessing for the ayahuasca before it was handed out to everyone in shot glasses. Drinking this sour brew was mind blowing. After an hour I saw energy particles and waves floating around me. I saw the energetic auras of the shamans and helpers as they moved around the room helping people. Visions of theories that I'd studied about quantum mechanics swirled in front of me as if I was watching an 8D movie. It didn't make any difference whether I had my eyes open or shut. Unanswered questions I had wrestled with were answered with a simplicity that felt easy to understand. But who gave these answers? I felt as if I'd been plugged into the source of everything and I was receiving downloads of important information.

Out-of-body experiences

Over a week, as each ceremony gave me different insights, I felt a strong connection with my consciousness and had my first out-of-body experience. If you've watched the movie *Avatar*, then you'll get a sense of what it felt like. I felt totally weightless and there was a joyful innocence that arose within me. I was able to see situations and people from a totally different perspective. I witnessed my great-grandmother's death and the anger from her unborn child. I saw the injustice that I'd unknowingly inflicted upon my daughter's father. I had always suppressed my judgement of my mother for her inadequate parenting. I was given an experience of what it felt like to be my mum and how she had never felt truly loved and accepted by her own mother. I saw how I had perpetuated this belief within her that she wasn't loveable, and I cried for hours at my own unjust treatment of her. I saw the way I had tried to control my own daughter in the name of love as I peddled my own beliefs for what would make her happy, rather than allowing her to find her own path to happiness. It was an enlightening few days.

The echoes of the aftermath

Months after the trip, I had a strong sense of deep change because I totally accepted that I am consciousness living in this space–time reality. Your logical brain often blocks expansion of awareness because it has been conditioned to believe certain things. If you accept and assume that the larger aspect of you is non-physical, you effectively enrol yourself onto an accelerated programme of evolution and growth. Having experienced an altered way of understanding life, I started to see how the tools and techniques that I had pioneered over my lifetime could be blended into a format that allows every individual to experience their true nature and their limitless potential as a creator of anything. When you can challenge how you have done things in your past and allow yourself to surrender to new concepts, new thinking and new ideas, then your consciousness becomes a real and important aspect of your journey through life. You begin thinking differently. You see everyone differently. Complex problems become simple signposts to freedom. When you dream at night, your consciousness is dominant. When you wake up in the morning, have you awoken or are you asleep?

Your magnetic thoughts

Every thought you have comes with a degree of emotional attachment. Your thoughts and memories are filed within your unconscious mind by order of emotional similarity. Every experience, memory or thought that contains an emotional attachment of fear will be filed together in a folder marked FEAR. If you have a thought that triggers some fear and you continue to dwell upon this thought for 15–20 seconds, you'll attract another fear-based thought. Now you've doubled your fear level in less than 20 seconds and other fear-based thoughts come whizzing into your consciousness. In a short space of time you've created a momentum of fear that is so intense, it's impossible to stop. Your day is on course for lots of fear-based experiences.

Breathing Space builds positive momentum

After waking up, I suggest that you do Breathing Space as soon as is practically possible to enable you to access a positive start to the day. At night when you sleep, your unconscious mind is busy processing everything from the day before. Sometimes that processing might not have finished. Breathing Space accelerates this overnight processing by helping you to release unhelpful emotions that have come to the surface. Your day then starts from a place of positive momentum, ensuring that the likelihood of you attracting more positivity throughout the day is significantly increased.

You are vibrational

As a non-physical consciousness, your thoughts create energy that cause a vibrational wave. You may have a favourite radio programme that requires you to tune into the specific broadcasting frequency. If you're on a classical music frequency, you can't hear pop music unless you change the frequency on your radio. You have to tune into the broadcasting frequency of your favourite programme to hear your favourite music.

You have a broadcasting frequency that is unique to you and is determined by the emotions you are feeling in the current moment. Sometimes you'll be aware of how you're feeling, and often you are unaware of the levels of negative emotion you have repressed in your unconscious mind. When you are angry, you notice people, situations or events that validate your anger. When you're feeling exhausted, you notice reasons that validate your exhaustion. You blame those external conditions for the reasons why you feel as you do and immediately cast yourself into victim mode. But unless you change your emotional state, you will continue to witness and experience that which you do not want to experience. To create any change outside of you requires you to change what's inside of you first.

The one thing for instant change

If you stop expecting things, people or experiences to be the catalyst for you to feel good and make feeling good your daily practice, then the transformation in your life can appear miraculous. You may think that you need perfect health, a wonderful relationship, an abundance of money and an exciting career to be happy, but in the absence of these factors they often become the source of unhappiness. If you're worried about not having enough money, you're vibrating on a frequency of *not enough money*. Feeling abundant and comfortable is a totally different frequency. You can't jump frequencies unless you jump your emotions. The more you focus on money, the more conscious you become about not having enough. Money, or a lack of money, isn't the issue. You've attached worry to the thought of not having enough money and this attachment will continue to keep you lacking money. Your outer reality always matches your inner reality. When you experience something in your external reality that isn't what you want, you are getting instant feedback that you need to change how you feel.

Ask yourself why you want more money. Most people will say that it makes them feel better in some way. If you change your focus away from money, because it triggers negative attachments, and focus on things that make you feel good, then you've created a frequency that's more positive. When people are made homeless because they have no money, their suffering perpetuates their awareness that they have no money. It's incredibly difficult for these people to switch their focus away from what they don't have when they're struggling to survive. But unless they change what they focus their attention on, their lives will never change. Viktor Frankl describes this point brilliantly in his 1946 book, *Man's Search for Meaning*. In the cruel and tortuous concentration camps, those prisoners who found something in their lives to feel positive about lived longer.

When life isn't going your way

It's easy to feel good with the sun shining or if you're sitting by the sea without a care in the world. It's easy to feel good when you're in the first flush of love or when you move into a new home. It's easy to feel good when you've just had your nails done or you've had a wonderful walk in nature. But life is full of ups and downs, and the real challenge is to feel as good as you can regardless of what is happening in your external world. This doesn't mean you can't be compassionate. If you have a friend who is depressed, you can't help them to get out of their depression by getting depressed alongside them. Two depressed people will increase the momentum of depression and you'll depress lots of other people along the way. Why would you do this to anyone, including a friend? There is a scientific theory that explains this phenomenon really simply. I remember when I was at school, taking part in science experiments. On one occasion we observed what happens when you drop two identical pebbles into water at the same time. The energy from both pebbles is shown as a wave and this synchronicity amplifies the energy of both pebbles. This is referred to as constructive interference. If you're feeling the same emotion as intensely as another person, then the emotion present within both of you increases. A positive example of this is when two people are in love. But if you're misguidedly wanting to show the other person how much you care by getting depressed as an empathetic response, then you'll both end up even more depressed!

Collective momentum

In 1895 Gustave Le Bon explained that behaviour observed in crowds could be attributed to individuals being lost in the collective nature of the group. From my perspective this is an example of the power of people aligning on the same frequency through a shared emotional experience. Look at crowd responses to riots, demonstrations, music festivals and football matches. The collective group's emotion builds the intensity of that emotion. To create a positive change within another individual or a group of individuals is to feel a positive emotion with greater intensity than the intensity level of their negative emotion. You have to find a way of perceiving your friend that causes you to feel a positive emotion. Whoever has the most intense emotional experience will influence the other person's emotions. When you turn on the news and watch the horrors and negativity, what reaction does it trigger within you? Regardless of how upset you get, it does not help humanity. Being upset just lowers your vibration and that's what people sense. You do have a choice. You can ignore those people, things or situations that trigger negative feelings within you. Many of my friends no longer watch or read the news. Or you can train your mind to detach the emotion from what you are observing. Many people practise daily meditation and this enables them to manage their emotional responses with greater wisdom. Or you can look for what's great about your friend or what's going well in a situation. When you change how you feel, then you change how others feel. Many people help themselves to do this by rewiring the way they think with positive affirmations and guided meditations.

Driving yourself too hard

Imagine driving in the outside lane on a busy motorway. You're speeding in an effort to outsmart your satnav because you're not going to get to where you want to go in time. From the moment you awoke that morning, your thoughts were sprinting across your mind trying to process all the activities and duties you needed to accomplish that day. You grabbed a coffee for a shot of caffeine and skipped breakfast so that you could respond to urgent emails. With growing impatience, you notice your fuel tank is almost empty and your driving speed has devoured fuel like a thirsty dog on a hot summer's day. Do you risk getting to your meeting without stopping for fuel or do you just accept that you're going to be late? Bizarrely you find it hard to decide. A simple decision but one that you feel impotent to make. Your knuckles are white as they clench the steering wheel, causing blue veins of tension to rise like scars that provide evidence of pain. You're perspiring heavily, even though you are in an air-conditioned car. Your shoulders and neck feel frozen under the burden of responsibility you continue to carry from one day to the next. On the motorway when you are driving at a hundred miles an hour you miss the surrounding scenery because you have to totally focus on what's ahead. A momentary lapse in concentration could cause a catastrophic accident. You know this, so the process of driving becomes tense and stressful. The minute you take your foot off the accelerator and switch down a gear, you find it easier to breathe. You notice fields of buttercups, trees that have witnessed centuries of unfolding events. Your body softens as you relax into the driving seat and breathe in the fullness of your life. When you slow down, you gain a rich perspective that is aligned with the truth contained within your heart. When you slow down, you are able to see what is really important.

Breathing Space slows you down

Breathing Space helps you to slow down and in doing so offers you a life that is easier to live and more rewarding. Your life, your body, your uniqueness is more precious than a multi-faceted diamond. If you can yield to the slowness of your true nature, then every moment holds the possibility for enhanced tranquility. When you breathe deeply, you rejuvenate your soul and find it easier to appreciate what a beautiful world you live in. When you stop sacrificing today for the illusion of tomorrow, you become an intentional creator of your own destiny. When you slow down you can embrace the ebb and flow of life. Once you stop rushing through life, you'll have more time for living your life. You'll be better placed to respond to every call that excites your spirit. It's your life, and it's the most precious possession you have.

7

WHAT IS BREATHING SPACE?

The great news about Breathing Space is that you feel better after just one short session. For many people this is a pleasant surprise and helps to keep your motivation levels high around consistently practising it. Apart from an instant sensation of feeling less stressed, there are a number of benefits that you'll notice within the first few days of practising Breathing Space. You will:

- Feel much more relaxed about life
- Notice improved cognitive function
- Have more clarity around what's important
- Experience increased energy levels
- Notice that your sleep quality improves
- Become more tolerant with people
- Find your mental health has improved
- Have increased self-confidence
- Experience improved personal relationships
- Possess greater self-awareness
- Feel more connected with nature
- Have glowing skin and brighter, fresher eyes
- Experience a healthier relationship with food.

Bizarre experiences

As you get into your Breathing Space practice, you may encounter a number of unusual experiences! Certain people have had an out-of-body experience, or they've seen beautiful colours. Some people see mystical shapes or have the sensation of moving quickly through a tunnel towards the light. Sometimes people tell me that they've received ideas or solutions to problems that they were previously unable to solve. Others report a surge in their compassion for others and have become more loving. Several people feel powerful and invincible. Others tell me that they've not felt stressed or angry for months, and couples who were on the brink of separation have fallen back in love with each other.

Everyone's experience is unique

Because you are a unique individual and there is no one else like you on the planet, your personal experience of Breathing Space will be unique. Your challenge is to remain open and neutral. As you gradually become more comfortable with this practice, you'll notice many different things that you didn't expect each time that you practise it. There is no guaranteed set of experiences because every Breathing Space practice is different. Over time, as you continue to practise Breathing Space, you'll notice that life feels easier; you are happier and more at peace and tolerant with what's going on around you. As you progress on to the longer sessions, you'll become so accustomed to feeling enlivened and invigorated that you might not consciously notice how good you feel. It's only if you don't do Breathing Space for a few days that you realise the impact it has been having on your physical and emotional wellbeing.

Your daily therapy session

Breathing Space is primarily a stressbusting technique. Imagine a dirty patio with layers of grime that has built up over the years. One day you decide to buy a pressure hose to clean your patio. At first the dirt looks like it's not budging, but with focused effort it soon softens, then releases. This is similar to how Breathing Space works. Every day it will search for a negative emotion that you've not yet processed and during the practice this emotion will soften and then release. Breathing Space works at progressively deeper levels. Initially Breathing Space clears negative emotions that are close to surfacing or are on the verge of being expressed. As you continue with Breathing Space, you'll gradually release more emotions that have become deeply buried within your unconscious mind. On occasions you may feel emotional, particularly when you first start practising Breathing Space. Welcome all emotions in the knowledge that they are coming to the surface for releasing. Over time, after clearing negative emotions, you'll notice that your Breathing Space sessions feel calmer. Every now and then, because your *pressure hose* has been working away on deeper, more stubborn, emotions that have become stuck for years, you'll experience the occasional intense emotional release. This is why it's beneficial to incorporate Breathing Space into your daily or weekly routine.

What is Breathing Space?

Breathing Space comprises four different processes that when blended together optimise the speed and impact with which you can release stress:

1. **Breathwork**. This type of breathing requires you to inhale and exhale through your mouth because

it's the quickest way to transport high amounts of oxygen into your bloodstream. This type of breathing creates a softening of old emotions that have become solid or frozen over time. It's a bit like being constipated! When your stools are hard they become stuck. A laxative is required to soften them so that you can comfortably *release your crap*. The breathwork step is like having an emotional laxative.

2. **Breath retention.** When you hold your breath for as long as feels comfortable, you start to influence your nervous system. This step switches you from the sympathetic to the parasympathetic nervous system that naturally calms you and restores your body's natural ability to repair, restore and heal. This process causes the relaxation of tight muscles, to allow the further release of old emotions.

3. **Primal releasing.** This step seeks to mimic neurogenic tremors that you may have witnessed in babies and young children. Notice how they express negative emotions with a fist-pummelling, foot-stomping tantrum that releases emotions. This is a natural way of keeping your mind and body stress free. Yet as you grew up you learned to control and bury this natural tendency.

4. **Rewiring your mindset.** With the growing awareness of neuroscience, your brain is malleable and highly responsive to change. Every thought sends an electrical signal that releases neurotransmitters that bind onto another neuron. This creates a circuit or path. The more you think a particular thought, the more you strengthen the path. Breathing Space changes negative thinking by building new, strong, empowering circuits.

These four steps are added to a variety of unique compositions that incorporate optimised technology to accelerate the speed of positive change.

Getting started

Breathing Space is a technique that is best practised lying down with a pillow or cushion supporting your head. You may want to place another cushion underneath your knees to support your lower back. Have a blanket or a light duvet handy so that you can cover up or throw it off if you need to. The process of releasing unprocessed emotions from your past will often cause a fluctuation in your body's temperature. Sometimes you'll feel cold and at other times you'll feel hot. Breathing Space can be practised in bed, on the sofa, on the floor or, weather permitting, outside on the grass. Because of the emphasis on abdominal breathing, you'll feel more comfortable wearing loose-fitting clothes, particularly around your waist. My favourite place to do Breathing Space is in bed in my PJs. But I live on my own. If you have a partner, you'll probably want to find somewhere else to practise, as it is an active and intense technique that can be intrusive if your partner is still asleep! Make sure that you have plenty of water handy and tissues. Sometimes Breathing Space can trigger a dry throat, an emotional reaction and congestion.

Best on an empty stomach

Breathwork is uncomfortable to do with a full stomach. You wouldn't exercise immediately after eating. But there is another reason why you should do Breathing Space with an empty stomach. It creates positive chemical changes in your body that will be hampered by the digestive process. There are three stages to digestion when your body breaks down food into smaller pieces, absorbs the nutrients needed by your body and then gets rid of the waste that your body can't use. When your body is busy digesting recently consumed food, you'll feel heavier and more sluggish. Your senses become dull and this will impair the efficacy of your Breathing Space practice.

Choosing a good time

When deciding upon the best time to schedule Breathing Space, it's important to do so at a time that works well for you. I'm a morning person and prefer to practise as soon as I wake. This means that I'm less likely to have my routine disrupted by the day's events. I like the feeling that I'm releasing any stress before I start my day so that I create a better, more productive and enjoyable day. But this might not work for you particularly if you have young children. Lunch times can work well; before you eat is also a good time because this helps to reduce any sluggishness that can often occur for many of us in the afternoon after we've had lunch. If you are feeling particularly anxious then the evening can be very helpful because it helps to release excess cortisol and adrenaline before you sleep. A word of caution: for some people, Breathing Space is overly stimulating and may energise rather than relax you – which is not conducive for a good night's sleep.

How often should you do Breathing Space?

Most people have acquired the tendency to suppress or repress old emotions that cause stress, tension and tightness in their mind and body. It's a really good idea when you're beginning Breathing Space to commit to doing at least ten minutes every day for 10 to 14 days. This clears away lots of unwanted emotions and gets you into a calm and grounded state. As with exercise, the more you practise Breathing

Space, the greater and faster the benefits. After the first two weeks, aim to do 60 minutes a week. You can divide this into three sessions of 20 minutes or two sessions of 30 minutes. You can even do six shorter sessions of 10 minutes each. You'll find your own routine because your self-awareness will be accentuated. If I don't do Breathing Space for three days, I feel more stressed and less compassionate. Even my family notices when I've not done it!

In the next chapter you'll be guided through a series of exercises and learn how to do each step of Breathing Space.

8

LEARNING THE TECHNIQUE

1. Breathwork

The next time you lie down and are feeling relaxed, scan your body and notice where you're feeling tense. Observe your breathing. When you inhale do you tense up your shoulders or can you breathe deeply into your stomach? Take a moment to reflect on what experiences and challenges you've experienced in your life. Are you at peace with what's happened in your past or are you still carrying emotional burdens? As you envision your future, what changes occur within your body? Your thoughts, your emotional burdens from the past, your perception of your future will be impacting upon the way you breathe. Sometimes the impact is subtle and sometimes it's more noticeable.

The story of your breath

The story of your life begins to change your breathing pattern. People with high anxiety exhibit a shallow, faster breath that keeps them disconnected from their feelings and causes over-thinking. People who are calm exhibit a slower, deeper breath that helps their life to flow better. The breathwork you do during Breathing Space helps you to access your entire respiratory system to fully oxygenate your cells so that everything in your body works more efficiently. Most people use less than half of their lung capacity and this deregulates their body's chemistry. Watch a tiny baby sleeping and you'll observe that their whole body is breathing – their back, belly and chest move together effortlessly. This natural ebb and flow to the breath usually starts to change when the story of your life begins to change your breathing pattern. Every trauma, every belief, every experience has danced along your breath, altering and shaping it until it is an accurate representation of the way you flow, or not, through life.

The main muscles involved in breathing are: the diaphragm; the intercostals located between your ribs; the scalene muscles in the neck; and the abdominals. When you are holding on to pain, either old or current pain, all of these muscle groups tighten. This constricts your ability to take deep breaths and creates more tension throughout your body. When you feel scared or anxious, there is a tendency to hold this fear in your digestive system. This causes tightness in your solar plexus, making it difficult to breathe deeply. The way you breathe is a metaphor for how you live your life. If your breathing is regularly constricted, shallow and uneven, then you restrict your life and flow of life force energy. Developing a more empowering breath pattern as a result of doing Breathing Space will create a miraculous transformation in many areas of your life. Your expanded breath expands your life force energy and purifies your awareness. Over time, your old internalised fear and pain, caused by destructive thought patterns, are transformed into love, compassion and equanimity, for yourself and with all living things.

The importance of pH balance

Hydrogen is present in all the fluids of your body and allows the toxins and waste to be transported and eliminated. It is responsible for keeping your joints lubricated and supports a healthy immune function. Your body has a natural pH balance that's slightly alkaline. The term pH represents the potential for hydrogen, and the ideal pH for your body is between 7.35 and 7.45. When your pH level is balanced, you experience mental clarity, high energy levels, a well-functioning immune system and have a lower risk of inflammation. When your body's pH is unbalanced, i.e. more acidic, your body is no longer in an optimal state. This can create constipation, bloating and fatigue. Breathing deeply is one of the most effective ways to alkalise your body. Taking full breaths that fill your belly has been shown to increase your oxygen intake, which cleanses your body on a cellular level, improving digestion by lowering stress hormones.

The breathing technique

Using a circular, diaphragmatic breathing technique, Breathing Space aims to remedy physical irregularities in your breathing cycle. This method of breathing introduces massive amounts of energy, in the form of oxygen, into your body. Each breath seeks out your unconsciously held negative patterns and trauma. Gradually, after repetitive breathing cycles, you start to reverse your breathing irregularities as you let go of mind/body afflictions. This direct breathwork innately triggers old emotional wounds, memories and trauma, for release. You inhale and exhale through your mouth because this is the fastest way to saturate your blood with oxygen. When you breathe deeply in, take your breath into your belly, expanding it as far as it will go. If you place one or both of your hands over your navel, it helps you to become aware of doing the practice correctly. You place emphasis on the inhalation, i.e. breathe in as deeply as you can.

To ensure that your mouth is fully open, take two fingers and see if they can fit comfortably in your mouth. Most people tend to close their mouth after a few minutes and miss out on much of the oxygen that creates the chemical shift. When you exhale, you imagine this as more of a relaxing or letting-go type of breath. Don't fully empty your lungs, you just release some of that oxygen. Once you've practised this type of breathwork for a few minutes, notice if you pause your breath after each inhale and exhale. Most people do. The knack is to create a continuous breath that just flows. Sometimes I find it helpful to visualise a circle. Imagine starting at the bottom of the circle. As you inhale, imagine drawing the circle up to the 12 o'clock point; then as you exhale, imagine drawing it down to the 6 o'clock point.

EXERCISE: Lie down and open your mouth wide enough to fit two fingers inside. Let's call this The Two Finger Check. Remove your fingers and place your hand on your stomach below your navel. Take a deep breath in and notice if your shoulders rise up. If they do, then relax them. Imagine your stomach inflating like a balloon on your inhale, then imagine pulling your stomach in towards your spine on the exhale. Take five of these breaths and notice how you feel.

Dealing with dizziness

The challenges that most people experience with breathwork usually disappear after seven to ten days. The first challenge is dizziness, which is caused by increased oxygen and lower levels of carbon dioxide. This is making your blood less acidic and causes a chemical alteration in nerve function that makes you feel light headed. This type of breathing temporarily throws out your ratio of oxygen to carbon dioxide, which starts to shift stagnant energy in your body. It's a positive indicator that you are altering your chemistry. If you experience dizziness initially, breathe normally for 15–20 seconds before continuing.

Dry throat

Another typical challenge with the breathwork section is a dry throat that can lead to coughing. Your body isn't used to this open-mouthed, deep breathing so your throat becomes dry quickly. This does improve over time, and the dryness can be significantly alleviated by drinking a glass of water before you start. Many people are unaware of how easy it is to become dehydrated by stress, central heating or air-conditioning systems, or not regularly drinking enough water. Your hydration level becomes evident when you start breathwork. This dry throat challenge should disappear after seven to ten days.

Feeling emotional

Your mind and body are interconnected. The emotions that you feel regularly, if unexpressed, will be held in your body. Old traumas and painful memories that you're consciously aware of, or not, can often be triggered through massage. The quickest way to affect your physiology is with your breath.

When you start the breathwork section you start to activate unprocessed negative emotions and they will rise to the surface. If you feel emotional during breathwork, that's a really good sign. With classical meditation practices it takes dedication and a lengthy period of time to clear negative emotions from your body/mind. With Breathing Space, you clear negative emotions at pace. During the first few weeks you may feel all types of different emotions. Rather than judge this as an adverse reaction, feel reassured that this is the equivalent of having an emotional colonic daily.

EXERCISE: Drink a glass of water. Lay down and open your mouth and do The Two Finger Check. Place a heavy book onto your lower stomach. Every time you inhale, raise the book by inflating your stomach. Take five of these breaths and notice how you feel. Remove the book then repeat this exercise, imagining you still have the book on your stomach. Try ten of these breaths and notice how you feel.

The challenge of deep breathing

For many people initially, the breathwork step is the hardest part of Breathing Space. If you've had a tendency to hold on to negative emotions around the throat and chest areas of your body, it becomes harder to breathe into your stomach. After a few Breathing Space sessions, you'll have released some of your body tension, so it feels easier to inflate your stomach. Some people like to move their head from side to side (inhale from the left and exhale to the right) whilst others like to keep their head still with eyes closed. Even if you simply breathe in this way for three to five minutes, you'll notice that your mood lifts and you'll feel happier and content.

2. Breath retention

At certain points during a typical Breathing Space practice, you're invited to take a big breath in and hold your breath for as long as feels comfortable. You do this with your mouth closed. The length of time that you can hold your breath reveals the degree to which you are psychologically in balance and your stress levels. When you feel calm and healthy, you'll be able to hold your breath for longer in contrast to when you're feeling stressed and tired. Over time, as you practise Breathing Space on a regular basis, you'll find that the length of time you can comfortably hold your breath increases significantly. When I first started to hold my breath, I could only do so for around 30 seconds. Now I can hold my breath for over two minutes and have on occasions held it for over three minutes. The benefits gained from breath retention are increased energy, calmness, resilience to stress, mental stability, a greater clarity and focus on priorities and goals, a closer connection to the body and a more focused attention to the present moment.

The autonomic nervous system

The purpose behind the breath retention step is to transition your autonomic nervous system from the sympathetic to parasympathetic to stimulate your body's natural healing ability. Your autonomic nervous system responds to environmental demands in two ways. It either stimulates your mind and body when responding to a real or imagined threat, or it works hard to maintain a homeostatic balance, allowing your body to rest, repair and heal. Your autonomic nervous system is divided into two major branches: the sympathetic nervous system and the parasympathetic nervous system. Your sympathetic nervous system puts your mind and body into a survival operating function and commands all resources to help you to survive. This is when your ability to plan, think objectively and communicate effectively is greatly impaired. Your parasympathetic nervous system works in a different way. It initiates a relaxation response, which lowers your heart rate and blood pressure and begins to engage in reparative and restorative functions. When your parasympathetic nervous system is in charge, your brainwave frequency moves from a beta into an alpha and theta frequency. This combination lets your brain know that it's time to heal, restore and repair.

Vagus nerve

During the breath retention section ~~of Breathing Space~~, your heart rate decreases and stimulates your parasympathetic nervous system. This improves heart function and boosts compassion. You'll feel more love towards yourself and other people. Stephen Porges, a contemporary neuroscientist, highlighted how the vagus nerve influences emotional expression. Charles Darwin first noted the impact of the vagus nerve in 1872 and hypothesised that emotional expression exchanges information with the brain and major organs such as the heart, lungs and gut. This is one of the first Western scientific acknowledgements of the mind–body connection! The vagus nerve originates in the brain stem and represents a series of nerve branches that relay signals between your brain and your body.

EXERCISE: Lie down and relax your body. Imagine asking your shoulders and your glutes to fully relax. Close your eyes and take a deep breath in through your mouth, then close your mouth for as long as feels comfortable. Notice how you feel and the different sensations in your body

Floating in your own consciousness

During the breathwork section you have absorbed lots of oxygen, which means that when you hold your breath your body has a large supply of oxygen and doesn't have the requirement to inhale it from the air. The initial sensation when you hold your breath after breathwork feels wonderfully calm. When you relax and surrender into this sensation, you'll be floating, weightless, within the space of your own awareness. You'll have the intense experience of the non-physical aspect of you, and this is a deeply meditative state for most people. Many people report that they feel they are rushing through a tunnel towards the light. Others report that they've seen beautiful colours and swirling symmetrical shapes. Sometimes you'll become aware of an important insight about your life or will be shown a solution to a long-standing problem. Early on when you begin the breath retention process, you may experience a tingling sensation throughout your body. This feels like a beautiful energy is seeking out and healing the aspects of you that require healing. Many people notice tears of joy streaming from their eyes as they feel an overwhelming sense of love and compassion.

EXERCISE: Lie down and open your mouth to do The Two Finger Check. Take 15 deep breaths based on the breathwork technique that you've just learned. Then, take a deep breath in through your mouth, close your mouth and hold your breath for as long as feels comfortable. Allow your eyes to close, relax your shoulders, relax your glutes (buttock muscles) and turn the palms of your hands upwards so they are facing the ceiling. This gesture signals to your brain that you are ready, open and receptive. You should be able to hold your breath for much longer this time. Notice what felt different and the sensations you experienced.

Techniques to optimise breath retention

There are a couple of things that will help you to optimise the benefits gained from the breath retention sections. The first one is to consciously relax your buttocks and shoulders because there is a natural tendency to clench and tighten these areas in particular. Any tightness in your body holds tension and activates your sympathetic immune system response, which is what you don't want! Allow the palms of your hands to face upwards because this appears to intensify the wonderful tingling sensation. I'm not really sure why this is but I suspect that this gesture conveys a message to your brain that tells it "I'm ready, I'm open, I'm receptive". During the passive sections that include breath retention, you may notice that your body temperature drops a little, which is why it's good to do this practice in bed so you can cover yourself with a light blanket or duvet.

Colours of healing

Over the years I have witnessed a phenomenon in my clients that seemed significant. During the breath retention process many individuals reported that they had seen different colours. After numerous investigative discussions, I realised that the colours observed were linked to the part of their body that was receiving healing based on the ancient wisdom of chakras. These are energy centres that are located throughout the body and are energy vortices or spirals that exist within the human subtle energy field known as our etheric body. Each vortex is a swirling mass that draws energy into its centre and moves it out as it transmits life force energy to and around the body. The word chakra comes from the Sanskrit and means 'wheel'. There are seven major chakras as well as other minor chakras. These swirling subtle energy centres are situated along the spinal column and are located between the base of the spine and the crown of the head.

Impact of blocked chakras on wellbeing

There are seven major chakras that are linked with each other and connected to parts of your cellular structure so you can receive, absorb and send life force energy. They are located around the major nerve ganglia and link with the glands of the endocrine system. The chakras vibrate at different frequencies as they transmit energy. Each is associated with a vibrational frequency, that for some people is witnessed as a characteristic colour. When you are overworked, tired, stressed and feeling out of balance, then these negative emotions become stuck and cause blockages in the chakras.

Interpreting colours

If you see a particular colour, check below to see what this means and the part of your body that was receiving balancing during the breath retention process.

1. **Root/Base Chakra** – associated with the colour red and located between your anus and genitalia. This chakra is about physical power and your connection with the Earth. When you feel grounded, you are able to deal with negative emotions more effectively. If this chakra is overactive, then you are likely to experience an obsession with money and possessions. You may be prone to angry outbursts and others may view you

as egotistical and controlling. If this chakra is underactive, then you may feel weak, vulnerable, lacking in confidence with a fear of abandonment. Physical illnesses associated with the Root Chakra include sexual dysfunction, tiredness and depression, issues with the prostate, reproductive systems and the bladder. When your Root Chakra is balanced you'll feel healthy and secure. Others will view you as authentic, kind and genuine.

2. **Sacral Chakra** – associated with the colour orange and located just below your belly button. This chakra is about confidence, your self-worth and your creativity. The Sacral Chakra is affected by the ease with which you relate and connect to others. If this chakra is overactive, then you may experience aggression, a reluctance around being alone, overeager in relationships and obsessed with sex. Others may describe you as driven, ambitious and manipulative. If this chakra is underactive, then you may feel overly sensitive, shy, timid and guilty about sex. Physical illnesses associated with the Sacral Chakra include kidney problems, constipation, impotence, menstrual disorders, pancreas issues and diabetes. When this chakra is balanced you will feel more creative, sociable, intuitive and attuned to your own feelings.

3. **Solar Plexus Chakra** – associated with the colour yellow and located at the top of your ribcage just below your sternum. If this chakra is overactive, then others will perceive you as a demanding and judgemental worrier. You may have a tendency to set high standards in a quest for perfection. Sometimes you will be too much 'in your head' rather than connecting emotionally. If this chakra is underactive, you're likely to feel

depressed, confused and worried, and these emotions will drain your confidence. You may feel insecure, needing constant reassurance and be overly concerned with what others think of you. Physical illnesses associated with this chakra are centred mainly around digestive disorders with physical and mental exhaustion. When this chakra is balanced you will feel empowered, strong, brave and confident.

4. **Heart Chakra** – associated with the colour green and located in the middle of your chest. When this chakra is overactive you may experience a 'martyr' attitude and be possessive and moody. You may feel out of control emotionally and demand much from others. When this chakra is underactive, you may feel repressed, indecisive, scared about letting go of relationships, getting hurt or being abandoned. You may feel unworthy of love and feel panic around the idea of being rejected. Physical issues associated with the Heart Chakra include heart and circulation problems, high blood pressure, asthma, tension, inability to sleep well and a weakened immune system. When this chakra is balanced you will feel unconditional love and a deep connection with nature and your spiritual purpose.

5. **Throat Chakra** – associated with the colour blue and located in your throat just in front of your 'Adam's apple' if you're male and in the middle of your throat if you're female. When this chakra is overactive you may talk excessively and have an inability to listen to others. You may feel uncomfortable with silence and others may describe you as being permanently on 'transmit'. If this chakra is underactive, you may stutter and

have a real fear of speaking. You may be scared about being judged or rejected. Physical issues relating to this chakra include thyroid imbalances, general throat problems, neck and jaw problems. When this chakra is balanced you will speak easily from your heart and will be able to listen beyond the words of others as well as to your own 'inner voice'.

6. **Third Eye Chakra** – associated with the colour indigo and located in your forehead just above the centre of where your eyebrows would meet. If this chakra is overactive, then you rely more on science, your intellect and what you are able to tangibly see on the surface. When the Third Eye Chakra is underactive, then you may feel sceptical about trusting your intuition. You may have a poor memory and have difficulty concentrating. Physical issues associated with this chakra include any problems in the brain, headaches, neurological disorders, mental disorders and learning disabilities. When the Third Eye Chakra is balanced you will elevate your Emotional Intelligence.

7. **Crown Chakra** – associated with the colour violet and located at the top of your head. When this chakra is overactive, you may experience a need to overthink and overintellectualise your experiences. When this chakra is underactive, then you may experience anxiety, confusion and a general sense of 'brain fog'. Physical illnesses associated with the Crown Chakra include genetic disorders, bone problems, paralysis and disorders of the nervous system. When balanced you will feel a deep sense of wisdom and more spiritually awakened.

EXERCISE: Review the definitions of the chakras and choose an issue that is relevant to you right now. Find the corresponding colour. Lie down and relax your body. Take 10 deep, open-mouth breaths then hold your breath for as long as feels comfortable. Consciously relax, close your eyes and visualise this colour. Once you're breathing normally again, reflect on the sensations you felt.

3. Primal releasing

All mammals have neurogenic tremors that are an inbuilt physiological response in order to release stress, tension and trauma. These consist of involuntary and rhythmic shaking that is witnessed in many animals. Some examples of this are that ducks flap their wings after a fight; a rapid and intense vibration is felt when holding a scared rabbit; and gazelles shake after escaping a lion attack. Animals just *shake it off*! This inbuilt way of releasing the high levels of cortisol and adrenaline associated with trauma and fear is a natural response within you. These tremors reduce overactivity in the hypothalamus/pituitary/adrenal axis to recalibrate your nervous system and bring your body back into balance. As we saw in Chapter Five, young children can suddenly appear calm when moments before they were screaming, pummelling their fists and stamping in a tantrum. From a young age you naturally released your emotions but may have been chastised by your parents – "Stop being a cry-baby", "Pull yourself together" – or you might have been threatened with dire consequences if you continued. As an adult you have probably suppressed this healthy way of getting yourself back into balance. The ability to proactively shake out your tension and trauma helps your body to remember that it does have a powerful way of releasing anything that no longer serves you.

Emotional freezing

Traumatic experiences at any age make you more hypersensitive to stress. You become easily upset by minor infractions and stressors. Your brain and body are frozen in an anticipatory stress response that continually triggers your amygdala, located within the temporal lobes of your brain. Its main job is to process emotional responses to calm the nervous system. But if you, like most people, are holding on to negative emotions, then your amygdala becomes overworked because you are feeling under continual threat. Human beings develop post-traumatic stress disorder (PTSD) because of frozen emotions. Long-term repression and suppression lead to excess energy being trapped in the body and results in chronic physical tension and mental and emotional distress.

General principles of primal releasing

Always release on the outbreath this is when you are exhaling. When you've completely exhaled, breathe in and release on your next outbreath. The intensity of your releasing is vital.

Imagine that you're a small child having a complete temper tantrum! Most people can be a bit tentative when they start doing primal releasing. After a couple of sessions, you'll feel much more confident when you discover that the greater the intensity, the more endorphins you activate. These are referred to as feel-good chemicals because they are connected to the pleasure centres in the brain. Most people experience a natural high and an elevation in their mood after primal releasing. It feels wonderfully cathartic! There are a number of different ways to release that can be used by themselves or together in different combinations.

Upper body boxing ball release

There are a number of rapid ways to release emotions and liberate your nervous system from fear. Whilst lying on your back, imagine a boxing ball in front of you. Raise your arms into a typical boxer's pose with your fists clenched, then pummel the ball as fast as possible. If you feel any strain on your arms, rest your elbows on your mattress and imagine beating a drum. With fists clenched, really connect with the natural rhythm that your body feels. These intense movements will cause your head to move. Many people hold lots of tension in the neck region, so releasing this tension feels wonderful. The faster you move your arms, the faster you'll be able to move your head from side to side. Stress is a major cause of jaw tension – are you aware that you clench or tighten your jaw when you're stressed, anxious or angry? Relax your jaw during the head movement and open your mouth slightly until you feel a vibrating sensation.

EXERCISE: Lie on your back and raise your hands up as if you are about to enter a boxing ring. Take a deep breath in and exhale as you release by pummelling an imaginary boxing ball, ensuring that your head and jaw are relaxed. Repeat for 30 seconds and notice the tingling sensation in your body.

Tongue release

Another way to release stress is by using your tongue. Your brain is neuroplastic, which means that it adapts to changes in behaviour, thinking and emotions. Scientists and doctors know that the tongue has a rich nerve connection to the brain. When you stimulate your tongue, you stimulate your brain function and create more flexibility in your behaviour and thinking. Consciously relax your tongue and let it *flop* out of your mouth as if you were about to pant like a dog. Then, and as you move your head from side to side let your tongue wobble in its own way. Initially it does make you feel a little bit crazy but can be deliciously liberating!

You can blend the boxing ball and tongue releases together for optimal impact.

Tongue trill release

Curl the tip of your tongue back slightly so it forms a cup shape in your mouth. Keep your tongue relaxed and let air pass through your mouth in such a way that it hits the tongue like a flag and flaps. If you add a bit of sound, you'll notice that you'll feel as if your tongue is vibrating. This vibration relaxes your jaw muscles and stimulates blood flow in the face and neck areas. This feels invigorating and can be used alone or in conjunction with the boxing ball release method.

EXERCISE: Add the tongue release to the boxing ball release and experience a deeper sensation. After 30 seconds, check in with how your body feels – are you able to notice the tingling sensation? Repeat the process again – this time replace the tongue release with tongue trilling. What way worked best for you?

The whispered scream

Screaming aloud is a cathartic experience because it's an intense way to release pent up fear. For many of us our family and neighbours might not be appreciative! You can get the same benefits by using a whispered scream. It's exactly like screaming but without the sound.

Leg releasing

When releasing tension from your legs, you have two main methods. The first is with legs straight – you move them up and down as quickly as you can. This is satisfying if you're practising in bed on a mattress but not quite as comfortable on a hard floor. An alternative option is to bend your knees and simply stamp your feet on the mattress or floor. If you want to optimise this releasing experience, add the tongue trilling release at the same time.

EXERCISE: Lie on your back and experiment with each type of leg release. Choose the one that feels optimal and do this for 30 seconds whilst adding the tongue trilling. Notice the difference in how you feel now.

Tingling sensations

After an intense primal releasing session, you are likely to notice a tingling sensation in different parts of your body. This is a sign that your life force energy has awakened and is flowing freely through your body. It is a really good sign! Most people feel this regularly during the first two weeks of their Breathing Space practice. Once you've become used to this sensation, your body accepts it as normal and aligns everything accordingly. This means that although you'll not feel this as intensely after a few weeks, it's still happening but you've grown accustomed to it.

Life force energy

Life force energy has many names depending on culture and beliefs. In Japan it's called *ki* (pronounced 'key'); in China it's *qi* (pronounced 'chee'); Indian yogis call it *prana*; and in Christianity it's referred to as *light*. Whatever we call it, there is a shared understanding amongst cultures that we are, at basis, life force energy, which maintains and heals us. The levels and ease of flow of life force energy in your body have an impact on your inherent healing ability. It helps to nourish every aspect of your body, supporting its vital functions and contributing to the healthy growth and renewal of cells. Because the amount of life force energy you absorb depends on many factors, you don't always replenish your supply of it. Lack of sunlight, stress, ageing, poor diet, depression and a lack of feeling grounded in the physical body are all factors in determining life force energy levels. When life force energy is high and flowing freely throughout your body, you feel healthier, stronger, fitter and more energised. You'll notice a surge in your confidence levels, you'll be ready to enjoy life more and you will be less prone to illness.

Headaches

Sometimes the primal releasing causes headaches. If you suffer from headaches or migraines generally, you may be putting too much pressure on yourself or are too self-critical. Breathing Space will be a powerful medicine for this and gives you a strong reason to persevere through the initial challenging sessions. It's likely that headaches are caused from a feeling of congestion. Too much *stuff* is being crammed into your consciousness. The quickest way to release this *stuff* is to blow your nose thoroughly during the primal releasing sessions. This has an immediate and positive impact. Your head feels lighter and more spacious and any pain has been *blown out* of your body. I experienced this personally during my trip to Costa Rica. The ayahuasca plant medicine was triggering my own *stuff* that was coming up to the surface for releasing. I had a constant headache that scared me because I suffered from migraines for years. I received a strong intuition to blow my nose regularly and my headache disappeared. Blowing your nose is another form of releasing your *stuff*.

Yawning

I've seen thousands of clients over the years and on one occasion I was working with a well-connected business leader who had various ancestral connections with royalty. He was a tall man with lots of natural gravitas and he had become very good at hiding his emotions. When we started my usual breakthrough process, instead of an emotional or physical releasing response he started yawning uncontrollably. At the time I didn't have the awareness or the experience to recognise yawning as another way that people release trapped emotions and blocked energy from their body. Yawning can also be an indication of a poor breathing pattern that is leaving excess carbon dioxide in the lungs. It took my own ayahuasca experience, when I yawned all night, to realise that yawning is a powerful releasing method and not just an indicator of tiredness or boredom!

Cold hands and feet

You may notice that during the first two weeks of practising Breathing Space your hands and feet get really cold. This is a sign that you're releasing past traumas that have created emotional numbing or emotional freezing. The temperature of your hands and feet will return to normal fairly quickly. Another 30 seconds of primal releasing usually resolves this.

Emotional releasing

When you begin to use your chosen primal releasing method you are likely to experience a surge of emotion as it rises up within you. That emotion is ready to leave you and is a really good sign that everything is working as it should. Sometimes you'll realise you're crying, even sobbing, and at other times you may find yourself laughing uncontrollably. Give yourself permission to go with whatever comes up for you and surrender to the releasing experience.

Nausea and bowel movements

Occasionally you may feel a little nauseous or experience the urge to go to the toilet. These reactions are rare when releasing but can happen particularly during longer sessions of 45 minutes or more. If you experience either of these, then slowly sit up. Usually this physical action stops the nausea and the need for the loo. But, if you need to go, of course you must go!

Go for it!

For many practitioners of Breathing Space, the primal releasing is their favourite part. Really go for it and allow your natural instincts to guide you. If you have a compelling urge to release in a different way to those suggested, trust yourself and do what feels good for you. During each Breathing Space practice, you'll notice that the intensity of your releasing begins to lessen. This is normal. Once you've released whatever your breathwork has triggered, it takes further sessions to get to other deeper layers of mental afflictions that require releasing. It's not just emotions that you'll be releasing; negative mindsets such as conceit, arrogance, sarcasm, pride and intolerance will also soften and release.

Spiritual awakening

Regular releasing causes a purification of your mind that brings with it a sense of interconnectedness with everything. At this level, you transcend your egoic mind and begin spontaneously feeling compassion and loving kindness towards everyone including yourself. This development naturally brings a growth in clarity of mind and wisdom. You may well receive spiritual insights, mystical revelations and have out-of-body sensations.

Surrender your fortress

Over the years, you have created walls of protection, built by your egoic mind to protect against the illusion of fear and vulnerability. In truth there is nothing to fear, because your true self is perfect. As Breathing Space softens your protective walls you'll feel an agitation of repressed fear. Your need for control comes from feeling vulnerable. If you allow yourself to let go, you move into a place of complete liberation from your fears. Once they have released, they've totally disappeared forever. As you continue to do Breathing Space, you'll receive a spiritual awakening and the old, egoic you will soften. During the first few weeks, because you'll be releasing lots of negative emotions, it's not productive to make life-changing decisions, set up new businesses or go into intellectual analysis and over-thinking. You need to transition through this phase as quickly as possible to access a state of calm. Only from the place of a calm, quiet and clear mind will you be able to connect with infinite intelligence and align to what's really important to you. You cannot help others until you've touched the centre of your loving nature. Breathing Space holds the potential to reconnect you to who you really are, at your core.

4. Rewiring and reprogramming

A belief is a thought pattern that you think on a regular basis to the extent that it has become habitual. Many of the beliefs you have will have been formed when you were younger and are no longer relevant or aligned with the adult you are now. Even if you are aware of your limiting beliefs, they have become so ingrained into your psyche that they cling on to you like a limpet grasps the rock face. The whole brain, when functioning correctly, is a phenomenal dance, coordinating 20 million billion bits of information every second. The human mind, using the brain as a tool, is capable of producing anything from a profound transcendental meditative experience to being triggered into fear or depression.

Changing your neural circuitry

The brain contains billions of neurons that communicate with one another through synaptic connections. A thought fires off an electrical signal from one neuron and neurotransmitters are released which then bind to receptors in another neuron. When you were learning how to read, your mother may have pointed to a picture of a bird as she said "bird" aloud. This started a neural circuit that linked the picture and sound together. The more times your mother did this, the stronger the connection. Now, every time you see a bird, the neural circuit in your brain is fired up and your immediate thought is "bird". Imagine walking through dense foliage for the first time. Initially there is no clear pathway. As you continue to walk the exact same way, the pathway becomes more defined. You are constantly creating neural pathways with your daily thoughts, which is why we find it easy to get into habitual ways of thinking and behaving.

Neural pathways are malleable so you can *eliminate* unhelpful neural connections by not thinking the same thoughts or behaving in the same way. Which means that you can create new, empowering neural pathways. This is why repetition is important to conscious learning. When you use your unconscious mind, you access the power and ease of a combine harvester that immediately carves out a wide pathway. Trying to create new pathways with just your conscious mind can be likened to scything the wheat by hand.

The unconscious mind creates accelerated change

After completing the breathwork, primal releasing and breath retention sections, you'll be in an altered state of consciousness and the pathway to your unconscious mind is wide open. At this point you are very suggestable. This is the perfect moment for rewiring and reprogramming your neural circuitry, which is done using a number of hypnotic techniques. You'll hear two voiceover parts when you listen to the guided tracks which are a key part of Breathing Space (more about these in the next chapter). One voiceover speaks to your conscious mind in abstract language that deepens your trance-like state and simultaneously the other voiceover speaks to your unconscious mind with positive affirmations. When listening to both voiceover parts together, your conscious mind is overloaded as it tries to make sense of both voices. This creates more deepening of your trance-like state so that your unconscious mind finds it easy to accept and act upon the positive affirmations.

Frustration around not understanding

Sometimes people feel frustrated because they can't process or make conscious sense of what is being communicated. The sooner you accept that what you are hearing cannot be understood, the sooner it will actually elevate your ability to receive powerful commands for easy and comfortable change.

Different people will hear different words and phrases. Your unconscious mind really loves you and is always on the lookout for ways to help you to feel better. Relax completely during this part and you may even fall asleep for a moment!

Each element is powerful in its own right

Each of the four elements that create Breathing Space is powerful in its own right. When blended together the experience is truly mind blowing and creates an immediate change in how you feel. Now for the icing on the cake – you're about to discover how technology accelerates the benefits gained from Breathing Space and why it adds a dimension that really does get you to a transcendent state quickly!

EXERCISE: Download the free Healing Hub app and, with headphones, listen to the Serenity 1 track. Notice how the music guides you through each step of Breathing Space. Listen to the affirmations part at the end and notice how you feel. Now play Serenity 1 again and this time participate in all the sections. Give yourself a few moments to scan your body and notice how you feel.

9

TECHNOLOGY INTO 'MINDOLOGY'

You can benefit from the first three steps of Breathing Space without any guided tracks. If this is your preference, then a typical daily session follows this simple structure:

- Breathwork – 20 open-mouth breaths from your stomach
- Breath retention – hold your breath for as long as feels comfortable/ up to 90 seconds
- Primal releasing – release using your preferred methods for 30–45 seconds
- Repeat these steps again
- Relax and breath normally for 60 seconds

If you want a deeper experience to optimise more benefits from Breathing Space, download The Healing Hub app and grab yourself some headphones. By using leading-edge technology, you can positively influence your mindset, your self-worth and your health and wellbeing. This exciting range of features creates another layer of emotional and physical healing that are contained within unique guided tracks.

Music is a vital component to Breathing Space because,

whilst each of the four elements has its own 'unique essence', it is the blend of these elements that really delivers such a powerful and enthralling experience. Music affects your psychological state of mind because it has the ability to evoke powerful emotional responses in listeners. Pleasurable music can trigger the release of neurotransmitters such as dopamine, which is associated with other forms of pleasure such as food, sex and drugs. Many studies have shown that listening to music is an easy way to alter mood and relieve stress. The dopamine influences other regions of the brain. Think of your brain as a computer system. The grey matter (nerve cells) of your brain is the computer and the white matter is the cabling that connects everything together and transmits signals. Your ability to enjoy music is linked to evidence showing that people who consistently respond emotionally to musical stimuli possess stronger white matter. This is important to overall brain health and cognitive ability.

Meet my musical family

My family are musical and gifted in their own way. My father used to play the piano and, although he never had a piano lesson in his life, his boogie-woogie kept me entertained for hours. My sister started playing a toy piano from the age of four and her natural talent won her a place at the Royal Academy of Music. She has performed with well-known artists and plays classical pieces with the same passion as she plays jazz and pop. Her partner is a real dude on the electric keyboard, her daughter Pippa sings, and her eldest son Jack went to the BRIT School for performing arts, to develop his natural talent as a guitarist. My brother has enjoyed a lifelong hobby of playing guitar and still performs in a band in his fifties. My daughter Rosie has a beautiful singing voice and composed and sang a wonderful song for me on my 55th birthday. When I started writing and recording meditations, it was an obvious choice to ask my sister to compose the music for them. It was a fascinating experience watching her accompany my meditations as she composed the musical pieces as she heard them.

Harry Valentine

It was my nephew Harry who gave the whole family the biggest shock, when he performed an enigmatic and brilliant piano composition at my dad's 80th birthday party. Everyone, including my sister (his mum), had no idea he was so musical. Over the years Harry saved hard to build his own mini recording studio and his passion for gaming has inspired a number of musical compositions that have earned him a big following on SoundCloud. Initially I felt concerned that Harry would struggle to create strong emotional pieces that would be appropriate for my audience. But after the first Breathing Space project, I knew that Harry's intuitive sense could translate my vision into emotionally charged music to heighten the listener's sensory experience. As a team, we regularly produce the guided tracks for Breathing Space and continually search for different ways to optimise the efficacy of our work.

Emotions have a rhythm

Rhythmic entrainment is a process whereby a powerful rhythm in the music influences the heart rate and, therefore, the emotional response of the listener. Variations in pitch and tempo also create different emotional responses. For example, a low pitch when an octave leaps downwards can trigger sadness and melancholy in contrast to a high pitch that generally creates positive emotional responses such as happiness, grace, triumph and serenity. Breathing Space creates a meditative state quickly, but when blended with rhythmically entrained compositions, this creates a multi-sensory experience. The breathwork tracks have a consistent and regular rhythm that enhances your ability to breathe deeply from the stomach. The releasing tracks use fast drumming sequences to activate negative emotions, particularly fear and anxiety so they can be released quickly. The breath retention tracks have a relaxing pace and tone that naturally quietens thinking and soothes the nervous system. The musical soundtrack becomes the guide for the listener's Breathing Space experience. The music ties everything together into a musical production that feels satisfying and rewarding.

Binaural beats

Binaural beats have a proven impact on altering your state of consciousness. This powerful technology has been built into every Breathing Space track to ensure that listeners, regardless of experience with meditation, can access a deep meditative state quickly. The healing experiment that I conducted with Hugo Jenks in 2012 showed me that a theta frequency binaural beat was the most appropriate for Breathing Space. I was further reassured by the scientific studies of Thomas Campbell, a nuclear physicist who recommends the daily use of alpha binaural beats to improve understanding of consciousness. For some people who think at speed, binaural beats can feel a little uncomfortable at first. If you experience mild nausea at first, remind yourself that your brainwave patterns are altering while you listen to Breathing Space. You are training your brain to slow the speed of your brainwave frequencies. The more you do Breathing Space, the quicker your brainwave frequencies adjust so that, after a couple of days, this phenomenal entrainment process is entirely unconscious. Most people don't hear the binaural beats used in Breathing Space. Some people hear them as a vague white noise that often feels muted in contrast to the overall experience.

Improving whole mind thinking

Sound is the energy things produce when they vibrate. Imagine banging a drum. The tight skin of the drum vibrates quickly and forces the air around the drum to vibrate as well. As the air moves, the vibrations from the drum spread outwards. The air inside your ears starts vibrating, which is when you perceive the vibrations from the drum as a sound. According to American researchers who conducted a study about the way newborn babies hear, your right ear is better than your left ear at receiving sounds from speech, whereas your left ear is more sensitive to sounds of music and song. Each half of your brain processes sounds differently because of differences in the brain cells in each side.

Left and right hemispheres

Your brain is comprised of two hemispheres that are separated by a bundle of nerves. The left hemisphere controls movement for the right side of the body, while the right hemisphere directs the left side. Each hemisphere has a different mental function. The right hemisphere, also known as the female brain, is the area that focuses on the abstract aspects of life such as intuition, clairvoyance, telepathy, empathy, creativity, receptivity, acceptance and dedication. The alpha frequency and the state of inner calm are created in the right hemisphere. The left hemisphere is more influential around reasoning, logic and control. It is also known as the masculine brain. Neuroscientists who have been inspired by the work of Nobel Prize winner and psychobiologist Roger W. Sperry have found that although the two hemispheres have different functions, they actually complement each other. I wanted to optimise this important understanding of brain function by changing the balance of sound at various intervals between your left and right ear. If I want to give your unconscious mind a powerful and positive affirmation, this will be optimised if I 'speak' into your right ear. If I want to evoke an emotion within you through a particular piece of music, I'll play it with more emphasis into your left ear. Harry and I refer to this process as 'panning' because we literally do sort and shift the auditory experience between both ears. You can only experience the effects of panning and binaural beats when you listen to the Breathing Space tracks through headphones.

8D Technology

During the early stages of trialling Breathing Space with a small number of people, I received an exciting WhatsApp message from Ian, who urged me to listen to a piece of 8D music through headphones. As a regular 'devotee' of Breathing Space, he wanted me to incorporate this effect into Breathing Space albums. It was a no-brainer, and I worked with Harry to determine the optimum places during a Breathing Space track when 8D technology would really enhance the overall impact. The intermittent use of 8D creates *fractionation* – a process that takes you in and out of trance, and thereby causes a deepening of the meditative state. Listening to Breathing Space tracks in 8D audio puts you right in the centre of the experience, giving you that euphoric feeling of being surrounded by the music and special effects. The music, different instruments, the binaural beats and the voiceover parts move around your head from side to side, back to front, and, for some people, it creates an out-of-body experience. 8D consists of a technical process whereby you record audio within a virtual spherical dome and split the output results through left and right channels. Harry arranges the recordings so that the sounds are coming from multiple directions around you. You need to hear it to believe it!

Creating a routine that works for you

Each Breathing Space album features the different steps: breathwork, breath retention, primal releasing and rewiring. There are three different duration times based on the time you have available:

- Track 1 is around 10–13 minutes
- Track 2 is around 20 minutes
- Track 3 is 30 minutes or longer

The longer tracks are more intense and work at a deeper level. Some people prefer to start with the shorter tracks because they are easier to fit into their daily schedule. Other people want to release as much of their stress as quickly as possible and opt for the 20-minute tracks. The longer tracks are designed for weekends and days off when you have more time available.

Your aim is to complete 60 minutes of Breathing Space each week. In the same way that you schedule exercise into your week, you can schedule Breathing Space to suit your routine. This might look like any one of the following options:

- Six days of 10-minute tracks
- Three days of 20-minute tracks
- Two days of 30-minute tracks

Choosing an album to suit your mood

Every Breathing Space album releases stress. Yet each album is created and produced to suit different emotional requirements. Some days you may want to feel courageous, resilient and strong. On other days you may want soothing and something calming. Each album describes the emotional mood and if there are particular albums that you really love then you can mark them as a favourite. I urge you to try as many of the albums as possible to create a freshness and anticipation with your weekly practice. I wanted to ensure that there are different themes and musical genres so you can curate your own programme of Breathing Space based on your individual preferences: sounds of nature, space travel, the story of Atlantis, magical kingdoms, urban rap, laid-back Sunday morning, shamanic drumming, folk and classical. These are just some of the themes we have used to create an emotional mood that speaks to your heart at the right time and in a safe space. Different composers, different voiceover artists, different sound effects all help to contribute to a full multi-sensory experience that feels wonderfully liberating.

Raising your vibrational frequency

The blend of emotionally arousing music, binaural beats, panning and 8D surround sound creates a powerful multi-sensory experience that, when combined with the four different elements, creates immediate change on many levels. Ultimately your vibrational frequency becomes purer so that you effortlessly align with more of what you want from life. The impact from each Breathing Space practice stays with you throughout the day. Over time you'll become so accustomed to feeling good that you'll wonder how you ever managed without it!

10

YOUR JOURNEY TO YOUR BEST LIFE

How are you feeling? Excited, apprehensive, curious? What can you expect as you begin your Breathing Space journey? Because it will be a unique journey of self-discovery towards the true and extraordinary you. As with any journey there will be twists and turns in the road. There will be moments of struggling up the hills of your mind as well as the exhilaration of the downhills.

Reactions from loved ones

The rewards from practising Breathing Space are plentiful. But as the changes begin to stir within you, it's typical to experience some friction from family, close friends and work colleagues. This is very normal and a strong indicator that you're making good progress. People who are around you regularly have become conditioned to your old energy frequency. When you begin to change, you transmit and receive information on a different, more positive frequency. This stirs things up for others until they naturally align with your new energy levels. Your consistent practice and commitment to feeling good will at some point rub off on so many people.

As you continue to practise Breathing Space, you'll experience emotional cleansing and physical detoxification. After years of excess information cluttering your mind and stressing your nervous system, you'll feel peaceful, balanced and calm. With equanimity you'll perform better, your decision-making faculty improves, and you feel more connected with others. Ultimately your awareness of what is truly important expands and gives you crystal-clear clarity about life.

Prepare to meet your shadow

Hidden in the dark, murky depths of your innermost thoughts resides a part of you that you have judged unconsciously as so bad, so damning, that you sent it into exile. This is your shadow self. This aspect of your personality is the part that you don't want to admit to possessing but is intrinsic to your evolution. Until you acknowledge and accept the darkest parts of you, then those parts will rise up in different aspects of your life. Only when you love and accept all aspects of yourself will you experience harmony, bliss and serenity. Breathing Space will activate your shadow self, bring it into your conscious awareness for releasing. Imagine a dark room full of shadows and outside of the room it's surrounded by light. When you open all the doors and windows, the room is illuminated by light and the shadows no longer exist. Breathing Space illuminates what was your shadow self.

Show love to your shadow

Over the years I have released lots of anger, but still felt ashamed of what behaviour my anger had triggered in my teens. It was only when I was able to fully love and accept this aspect of myself that I liberated myself from my negative judgement of my shadow. I had a dream that I was being chased through a dark wood. The ground was uneven and everywhere looked the same. I was lost in a forest of tall trees. I was terrified to look back and see who was chasing me. When I finally looked behind me, I saw my shadow self, and she was crying out for me to love her. When you can acknowledge your most reviled parts with love in your heart, you'll notice that your shadow stops haunting you. Breathing Space brings up your shadow, helps you to accept and love it, and with that you have released it. This is a healing process that is amazingly cathartic.

When you develop a relationship of love towards yourself and are feeling safe, calm and supported, you feel in flow with life. You feel connected and compassionate to other people and to nature. Your senses appear wakened from a deep, nourishing sleep so that small details catch your attention and give you a warm glow in your heart. Ideas flow freely, inspiring visions, next steps and revolutionary thoughts that just resonate with you. As you let go of your stress you'll access a greater feeling of humanness. I remember reading the poem 'Desiderata', written by Max Ehrmann in 1927, and the following lines really jumped out at me:

> *You are a child of the universe, no less than the trees and the stars; you have a right to be here.*
> *And whether or not it is clear to you, no doubt the universe is unfolding as it should... With all its sham, drudgery, and broken dreams, it is still a beautiful world.*

To increase your joy you don't need to learn anything new. You simply have to feel comfortable being you, connect with your emotions and find purpose and personal meaning in your everyday life. It takes real courage to remain true to who you really are inside. Years of environmental conditioning often stops you from honouring your softer and therefore more vulnerable side. Breathing Space liberates you from emotional pain so you can experience euphoria at the sheer sensation of being alive. In the same way that you will never forget how to ride a bike, emotional freedom and happiness is your birthright; it is a natural state that is within you, just waiting to be awakened.

As I reflect on some of the turbulent events from my youth, I see that every difficulty gave me the opportunity to experience a new better facet of my character. Every challenge successfully overcome enabled me to experience a higher, better version of myself. To connect and listen to your core self requires courage to face the demons from your past, in the knowledge that they can no longer hurt you without your permission. You can't force happiness; you can't fake joy. You simply have to allow it. In my view, the legacy of your life is unfolding just as it should. The better you feel, the more positive influence you will create on other people's lives. When you are brave enough to live in your truth you carve out paths for others to do so as well. My greatest wish for you is that you find the courage to let go of anything that stops you from being your true authentic self. Because when you are being you and you love what you do, then you really are living your best life.

Join our growing community of Breathing Space subscribers at The Healing Hub and let us support you in your own Breathing Space journey. Use the code **SBYL21** to receive an instant £40 reduction from a premium annual subscription. **www.thehealinghub.uk**

KEY PEOPLE, EVENTS AND TERMS

- *Active mindfulness* is reconnecting with our bodies and the sensations they experience. It uses a simple activity through which to focus awareness.
- *Adrenaline* is a hormone secreted by the adrenal glands that increases rates of blood circulation, breathing and carbohydrate metabolism, and prepares muscles for exertion.
- *Ayahuasca* is a hallucinogenic plant medicine used for spiritual purposes by Amazonian tribes that leads to an altered state of consciousness.
- *Beachyjax* is a healing hub and retreat located on the edge of a nature reserve in Honley, Huddersfield.
- *Big Apple Experiment* was founded by Nikki Owen in 2010 to demonstrate the impact of directed intention on physical reality.
- *Binaural beats* occur naturally in the brain. A different sound (tone) frequency is sent to the right and left ears through headphones. Upon hearing the two different frequencies, the brain interprets

one consistent, rhythmic frequency, known as a binaural beat.
- *Bohr, Niels (1885–1962)*. Danish physicist, who won the Nobel Prize in Physics in 1922 for his contribution to understanding atomic structure and quantum theory.
- *Brainwaves* are produced by synchronised electrical pulses from masses of neurons communicating with each other. Brainwaves are detected using sensors placed on the scalp.
- *Consciousness* is awareness and sentience of internal and external existence.
- *Cortisol* is often called the stress hormone because of its connection to the stress response.
- *Dopamine* is known as the feel-good neurotransmitter – a chemical that ferries information between neurons. It boosts mood, motivation, attention and helps to regulate emotional response.
- *Double-blind trials:* in these neither the patients nor the researchers know who is getting a placebo and who is getting treatment. This removes the impact of belief from medical trials.
- *Electroencephalogram (EEG)* is an electrophysiological monitoring method to record electrical activity of the brain.
- *Ego* is one of the three constructs in Sigmund Freud's structure model of the psyche.
- *Emotional Freedom Techniques* is a form of counselling intervention that is best known through Gary Craig's *EFT Handbook*, published in the late 1990s.
- *Endorphins* are hormones secreted by the brain and nervous system which inhibit the sensation of pain and can produce feelings of euphoria.

- *Epigenetics* is the study of changes in gene expression or cellular phenotype, caused by mechanisms other than changes in the underlying going sequence.
- *Fire-walking* is the act of walking barefoot over a bed of hot embers. It's been practised by many people and cultures with the earliest known reference dating back to Iron Age India *c.*1200 BC.
- *Flow state*, also known as being *in the zone*, is a mental state in which a person performing an activity is fully immersed in a feeling of energised focus, full involvement and enjoyment in the process of the activity.
- *Foveal vision* is vision that arises from stimuli falling on the macula lutea of the retina. The foveal system of the human eye is the only part of the retina that permits 100% visual acuity.
- *Fredrickson, B.L., PhD.* Leading scholar within psychology, affective science (the study of emotion), and positive psychology.
- *Genetic determinism* is the idea that most human characteristics – physical and mental – are determined at conception by hereditary factors.
- *Hedonic treadmill:* the pursuit of material possessions and experiences under the incorrect belief that they will bring lasting happiness.
- *Homeostasis* is the tendency to maintain internal stability.
- *Hypnagogic* is a state of drowsiness that makes us more suggestable.
- *Iceberg analogy*: this idea by psychologist Sigmund Freud (1856–1939) states that the mind, like an iceberg, has a small visible conscious area and a large hidden unconscious that guides actions and thoughts.

- *Immunology* is the study of the immune system that protects us from infection through various lines of defence.
- *Infinite intelligence*, according to Napoleon Hill, is the force that gives order and origin to everything in the entire universe. It is the prime source, the first cause of everything that comes into existence.
- *Jung, Carl Gustav (1875–1961)*. Swiss psychiatrist who founded analytical psychology and first coined the 'shadow' as a concept.
- *Kundalini yoga* derives from *kundalini*, defined in Hindu lore as energy that lies dormant at the base of the spine until it is activated and channelled upwards through the body.
- *Matrix Reimprinting*, developed by Karl Dawson, is a technique that connects people to past traumas and enables positive transformation.
- *Nervous system:* this has two components, the central nervous system and the peripheral nervous system.
- *Neurogenic tremors* are innate to all mammals and are the central nervous system's innate way of discharging excessive tension through rapid muscle contraction and relaxation of tremors to calm the body down from an over-excited adrenal state.
- *Neuro-linguistic programming (NLP)* is an approach to communication, personal development and psychotherapy created by Richard Bandler and John Grinder.
- *Neuron* is a nerve cell that sends and receives signals from the brain.
- *Neurotransmitters* are chemical messengers in the body. Their job is to transmit signals from nerve cells to target cells.

- *Nocebo effect* is a negative reaction caused by a belief that something will harm you, for example when a doctor tells you a surgery could have negative results.
- *Norephedrine* is a substance released from the ends of sympathetic nerve fibres and increases the force of muscle and heart contraction.
- *Oster, Dr Gerald.* Biophysicist who in 1973 presented a paper 'Auditory beats in the brain' in *Scientific American* that sparked further research into binaural beats.
- *Oxytocin* is a hormone normally produced in the hypothalamus and released by the posterior pituitary. It plays a role in social bonding, sexual reproduction, childbirth and the period after childbirth.
- *Peripheral vision or indirect vision* is vision as it occurs outside the point of focus.
- *Placebo effect* describes a psychological or psychophysiological improvement attributed to therapy with an inert substance. If individuals believe the substance will help them, then it will.
- *Psyche*: defined by Freud as including three entities of mental function: the id, ego and superego.
- *Quantum physics*, also known as quantum mechanics and quantum theory, is a fundamental branch of physics which deals with physical phenomena at nanoscopic scale that explains the behaviour of matter and its interactions with energy on the scale of atoms and subatomic particles.
- *Reiki* is an alternative energy healing system that allows the transference of universal energy to encourage emotional and physical healing.
- *5Rhythms* is a movement meditation practice

devised by American dancer and musician Gabrielle Roth (1941–2012) in the late 1970s. It draws from indigenous and world traditions using tenets of shamanism, ecstatic, mystical and Eastern philosophy.
- *Rhythmic Entrainment Intervention* is a music medicine therapy programme utilising recorded hand drumming rhythms to stimulate the central nervous system and improve brain function.
- *Serotonin* is a naturally occurring substance that functions as a neurotransmitter to carry signals between nerve cells throughout the body. It helps to regulate mood and behaviour.
- *Shadow* is based on Jungian psychology and is an unconscious aspect of the personality that has been repressed and hidden from conscious awareness.
- *Spirit animal* is characterised as a teacher or messenger that comes in the form of an animal and has a personal relationship to an individual.
- *Synaptic connections* are brain structures that allow the neurons to transmit an electrical or chemical signal to another neuron.
- *Testosterone* is the primary male sex hormone and anabolic steroid.
- *Time Line Therapy*™ involves treatment at an unconscious level and allows a client to surrender negative emotions linked to the past. Developed by Tad James PhD in the 1980s.
- *Unified field theory:* pioneered by Albert Einstein (1879–1955), this describes any attempt to unify the fundamental forces of physics between elementary particles into a single theoretical framework.
- *Vajrayana Buddhism* is a form of Mahayana

Buddhism that originated in northern India around the 5th century CE, took root in Tibet in the 7th and 8th centuries and then spread across the Himalayan region, and is now practised globally.

BIBLIOGRAPHY

- Biali, S.M.D. (17 April 2018) '6 Ways That Nighttime Phone Use Destroys Your Sleep'. *Psychology Today*
- Campbell, T. (2015) *The Complete My Big Toe Trilogy; Unifying Philosophy, Physics, and Metaphysics*. Lightning Strike Books
- Cherry, K., medically reviewed by Block, D.B, MD (10 December 2019) 'How Listening to Music can Have Psychological Benefits'. *Very Well Mind*
- Corona, V. (1989) *Tahitian Choreographies*
- Dawson, K. (2010) *Matrix Reimprinting using EFT: Rewrite Your Past, Transform Your Future*. Hay House UK
- Doghealth.com – Hearing in Dogs
- Dolan, A. www.breathguru.com
- Fisher, N. (2 November 2015) 'Is Your Tongue The Key to A Neuroscience Breakthrough?'. *Forbes*
- Fitzgerald, J. (2012) 'Water Dehydration Causes Disease'. The Energy Circuit, Inc
- Frankl, V.E. (1924) *Man's Search for Meaning*. Penguin Random House

- *Gaia* Staff (13 March 2020) '5 Methods for Energy Healing'. *Gaia*
- Goleman, D. (15 October 1991) 'Happy or Sad, a Mood Can Prove Contagious'. *New York Times*
- Harvard Medical School et al. (23 June 2014) 'Stress causes damage to the heart study finds'. *Nature Medicine*
- Hill, N. (1937) *Think and Grow Rich*. The Ralston Society
- Institute for Creation Research (2007) 'The Amazing Jewel Beetle'. http://www.icr.org/articles/view/3268/233/
- Ivtzan, I., PhD. (11 March 2016) 'Dangers of Meditation'. *Psychology Today*
- Kapadiya, B. (17 April 2020) 'Quantum Mechanics and Double Slit Experiment'. *Physics Only*
- Knapton, S. (22 June 2014) 'How stress damages the heart'. *Telegraph*
- Le Bon, G. (1896) *The Crowd – A Study of the Popular Mind*. Dover Publications
- Lipton, B.H., PhD, *The Biology of Belief: Unleashing the Power of Consciousness, Matter & Miracles*. Hay House Publishing
- Lorenz, E. (1963) 'Deterministic Nonperiodic Flow'. *Journal of the Atmospheric Sciences*
- Marsden, R. (23 June 2014) 'Proof that stress really does cause heart attacks: Adrenaline can increase white blood cell production which can cause ruptures'. *Daily Mail*
- Maslow, A. (1943). 'A theory of human motivation'. *Psychological Review*
- McTaggart, L. (2008) *The Intention Experiment: Use Your Thoughts To Change the World*. HarperElement
- Melina, R. (31 January 2011) 'What Animal Has The Best Sense of Taste?'. *Live Science*

- Mosely, M., Dr. 'How Fear Affects Your Immune System Life Event, Stress, and Illness'. https://www.ncbi.nlm.nih.gov/pmc/articles/PMC3341916/
- MRC Centre for Global Infectious Disease Analysis (June 2020) Report 28 – Excess non-COVID-19 deaths in England and Wales between 29th February and 5th June 2020.
- Nicholas, S. (March 2010) 'Could talking to an apple help you become more beautiful?'. *Daily Mail*
- Niraj, N., MPharm, AKA The Renegade Pharmacist (April 10, 2017) 'The Benefits of Holding Your Breath'.
- Ofcom (2017) International Communications Market Report
- Oster, G. (1973) 'Auditory beats in the brain', *Scientific American*
- Owen, N. (1992). *Nicola – A Second Chance to Live*. Transworld Publishing
- Owen, N. (6 June, 2020) 'Review of Results of Breathing Space'. Roche
- Owen, N. (July 7, 2020) 'Review of Results of Breathing Space'. Goodwood
- Peale, N.V. (1952) *The Power of Positive Thinking*. Prentice Hall
- Peck, M.S. (1978) *The Road Less Travelled*. Arrow Books
- Preece, R. (2006) *The Psychology of Buddhist Tantra*. Snow Lion
- Pierce, T.H. (2004) *Outsmart Your Cancer; Alternative Non-Toxic Treatments That Work*. Thoughtworks Publishing
- Rakhimov, A., M.D. (5 August, 2019) 'Buteyko Technique: Evidence of Hyperventilation in Chronic Diseases'. www.normalbreathing.org
- Simons, D. and Chabris, C. (1999) 'Invisible gorilla

test and inattentional blindness'. www.theinvisiblegorilla.com
- Tims, A. (24 July 2010) 'The secret to... improving your concentration'. *The Guardian*
- Toffler, A. (1984) *Future Shock*. Turtleback Books
- University at Albany (22 June 2007) 'Psychologists Attribute Yawning to The Need To Cool The Brain And Pay Attention'. *Science Daily*
- PNAS (5 May 2014) 'Voluntary activation of the sympathetic nervous system and attenuation of the innate immune response in humans'. *Proceedings of the National Academy of Sciences of the United States of America*
- Wallace, B.A. (2012) *The Seven-Point Mind Training*. Snow Lion
- Wallace, B.A. (2011) *Minding Closely. The Four Applications of Mindfulness*. Snow Lion
- Wallace, B.A. (2007) *Hidden Dimensions. The Unification of Physics and Consciousness*. Columbia University Press
- Watson, K., medically reviewed by Murrel, D., M.D. (14 August 2018) 'Sinus Headaches'. Healthline

Unconscious Mind references:

- https://www.psychologytoday.com/us/blog/out-the-ooze/201801/the-freudian-symbolism-in-your-dreams
- https://www.verywellmind.com/what-is-the-unconscious-2796004
- https://www.britannica.com/science/information-theory/Physiology
- https://www.psychologytoday.com/us/blog/what-

doesnt-kill-us/201908/what-is-the-unconscious-mind
- https://www.britannica.com/science/information-theory/Physiology
- https://www.simplypsychology.org/unconscious-mind.html

ACKNOWLEDGEMENTS

Jacqui Cooper, you encouraged me to write daily. I love the rituals we did together that added a 'specialness' to the momentous task of writing a book.

Sue Skinner, your eagle eye is always appreciated. The discussions we had over some of the text really helped me to convey complex subjects simply.

Harry Valentine, my nephew. Your phenomenal talent to compose emotionally evocative music is extraordinary. You continue to surprise me with your ability to create a huge range of styles and moods. You are an exceptional young man.

To those of you who bravely pioneered Breathing Space during its embryonic state and gave me really helpful feedback. Particularly: Ian Teagle, Wendy Shand, Steve McConnell, Carrie Oliver, Karan Tattersfield and Maxine King.

Claire Pankhurst, you and your marketing team have created the bridge that has allowed me to share my work with the masses; I am truly grateful. Jane de Vos, Santiago Pilgrim, Matt Eamer, Sarah Smith and Andy Mildner, I couldn't have written this book without your support over the years.

Robert Wagner has transformed the work I have been doing, and I am grateful for his commercial wisdom and total belief in my stressbuster techniques.

ABOUT THE AUTHOR

Nikki J. Owen is a stressbusting expert and has helped over 2,000 individuals release their stress over three decades. She believes that any individual can live their best life when they are no longer burdened by stress, anxiety and overwhelm. Nikki loves walking in nature in her hometown of Sevenoaks, Kent and is the author of four published books. She practises Breathing Space every day.

For more information about Nikki's stressbusting techniques, visit:

www.thehealinghub.uk

Printed in Great Britain
by Amazon